CARLSON WADE'S NATURAL FOODS CROCKERY COOKBOOK

by Carlson Wade

Weathervane Books • New York

Contents

Copyright © MCMLXXV by Carlson Wade
Library of Congress Catalog Card Number: 75-10570
All rights reserved.
This edition is published by Weathervane Books
a division of Imprint Society, Inc., distributed by Crown Publishers, Inc.
by arrangement with Drake Publishers, Inc.
a b c d e f g h
Manufactured in the United States of America

Introduction

YOU ARE mighty interested in nutrition, flavor, and economy in cooking and eating foods. Now, thanks to the creation of a new appliance, the crockery pot (also known as a slow cooker), all three are yours. Slow crockery pot cooking is the new, exciting way to get more vitamins, minerals, and natural juices from all of your cooking. It's the way to enjoy food that's top in nutrition and has better flavor than you could ever get by boiling or frying.

You'll be thrilled at the tender, tasty meals you can create using economical cuts of meat, and your crockery pot cooks all day for less than five cents. What better way to save on you food budget — and conserve electricity, too.

The slow cooker gives you carefree cooking. There's no need to remain imprisoned in your hot kitchen (it's not so hot with the crockery pot), watching the meals. You need not worry about overcooked foods for late arrivals. The beauty of the crockery pot is that with its slow simmering method foods just cannot be overcooked. Your crockery pot turns out deliciously perfect meals — unattended. Nutritionally, the slow method seals in precious vitamins, minerals, protein and keeps them from evaporating. Slow cooking is the natural way to enjoy the best of the nutrient power in the food that might otherwise be "cooked away" by ordinary methods.

Imagine this: during tests, I simmered chicken and vegetables continuously for *30 hours*. Of course, this was longer than necessary, yet they were still intact and delicious to eat.

You will love having a crockery pot in your kitchen. It promises to be a flavorful change from what you're used to. For enjoyment at its best, may I suggest as a starter, pot roast or Swiss Steak? With a crockery pot in your kitchen, you can cook all day...and be away!

The recipes in this book represent the many categories of foods you can prepare with ease and confidence. Because the crockery pot is so versatile, you'll want to adapt some of your own favorite recipes. I've prepared a guide (see Chapter Three) to make things simpler for you.

Have fun cooking with your crockery pot slow cooker. You will discover a new world of eating pleasure and saved time. Your guests will hail you as a creative chef...when your crockery pot has done most of the work! So enjoy...enjoy...!

...CARLSON WADE

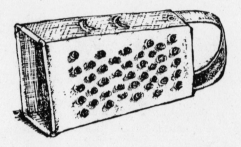

CROCKERY COOKBOOK

Chapter One
Let's Get Acquainted With Your Crockery Pot

REMEMBER THE big-bellied bean pot that sat for hours and hours, simmering tough ingredients to a mouthwatering tenderness? Perhaps you're too young to remember the flavor and juiciness of Grandmother's specialties. Part of the secret of her success was long, oh-so-slow cooking. She had a warm spot at the back of her cookstove that held foods at the perfect low temperature for day-long cooking. Well, now that old-fashioned stoneware pot has become the latest cooking utensil—updated so it fits right into modern kitchens, cooking habits, and current tastes.

Today, it is known as the *slow cooker* or the *crockery pot*. It comes equipped with its own electric heating unit. It can cook roasts, casseroles, soups, cereals, breads, vegetables, and, of course, beans. It is the joyful way to cook in our Space Age.

In recent years, the pace of our lives has accelerated to such an extent that we've lost out on the tasty goodness of old-time cooking. With the new electric crockery pot, we can cook meals that seem to belong to the unhurried past with the ease and convenience that's in tune with the jet age. If nostalgia nudges you to turn back the calendar every now and then, you'll love the electric crockery pot. It cooks and serves all your favorites in true country-kitchen style, bringing the aromas and flavors of yesteryear to your table.

"Slow cookers," as the new breed of appliances is called, prepare foods by cooking them at low heat (approximately 150°F. to 300°F.) over a long period of time—often eight, ten, even sixteen hours. The heating element encircles a heatproof cooking pot big enough to accommodate a pot roast or nearly a gallon of stew. The heatproof cover helps seal in flavors. But most important...you can set your slow cooker to a time schedule and *let it cook all day without looking.*

When the electric base gently transfers heat to the stoneware pot, foods are "simmer cooked." You'll find no better way to prepare old-fashioned baked beans, split pea soup, hearty stews, and chunky chowders! Equally inviting are other main dish specialties that benefit from slow mingling of flavors—chili, chop suey, spaghetti. It's an early-morning greeter, too. Use it to cook "real" oatmeal or a fruit compote made with prunes and apricots. The stoneware pot by itself can be used in the oven for favorite casseroles, and between cooking sessions, use it as a cookie jar on your kitchen counter!

What makes the crockery pot so delightful? In a word—convenience. Busy housewives, working women, fathers, sisters, brothers, even singles, can put a meal in the crockery pot and go about the business of the day. If your family eats in shifts, then the crockery pot is for you. Early, late, or right on time, each family member will find his serving perfectly cooked, warm, and flavorful. There's no problem if the cook comes home late either, because an hour or two of extra cooking in the crockery pot won't burn the food, only make it more tender! So forget about watching meals as they cook. Forget about that nagging question: "Will everything and everybody be ready at the same time?" And after dinner, there's no need to worry about lengthy scrubbing. Most crockery pots are planned so that the stoneware pot can be lifted easily from the electric base for quick, safe cleaning. Cook slowly; clean up fast: a nice mingling of the old and the new.

So you can cook in the "way of today" and still get taste-tempting dishes reminiscent of Grandmother's. And your slow cooker does great things for bargain-priced meats. The cheaper meats are best when cooked long and slow. Most of us, before we had a crockery pot, couldn't afford to stay at home all day watching stews and soups simmer on the stove.

Now we can pop foods into the crockery pot and take off for the day. Generally, food does not have to be watched, stirred, or turned during cooking. Often, you can put all the ingredients into the crockery pot at the same time, because vegetables simmered slowly do not overcook as they may do when boiled.

Your crockery pot saves money in another way, too—it costs only a few pennies for a full day's cooking. *Because most crockery pots are low-wattage appliances, the operating costs are low. A day's use of the crockery pot slow cooker costs less han a nickel!*

Simply plug it in and fill with the makings of a dish. You will enjoy a multitude of foods—easy-on-the-budget main dishes, savory soups and stews, taste-tempting beans, cereals and puddings, party appetizers—even hot beverages! Then set it and forget it! You can tend to other tasks, even go out for the day, while your crockery pot slow cooker minds the meal. It keeps a constant watch on the right cooking temperature. Then, as a food warmer and server, it maintains a steady warmth that keeps dishes piping hot for hours.

The crockery pot promises downright *good* eating. It's ideally suited to homespun family meals, national and regional delicacies, and fancy "company's a-comin'" dinners. Right on hand to greet early arrivals at the table, it also comes to the rescue of famished late arrivals; and it's always there for those who like to linger over good food and conversation. You will have fun discovering the "new-fashioned" dimension of slow cooking!

There are many different crockery pots available. A typical cookpot may be made of a combination of materials. The outside may be fashioned out of baked enamel, cast aluminum, a plastic such as Lexan, or stoneware, a heavy, porous pottery reminiscent of the old-time crock. Frequently, the inside of the pot (the cook well) is coated with a non-stick material, usually Teflon, or with heat-resistant glass or stoneware. Stoneware has advantages and disadvantages. It helps retain the natural juices and flavors of food, but is considered more vulnerable, in comparison to other materials, to damage from sharp knocks or sudden temperature changes.

Many crockery pots come with a removable inner lining which makes cleanup much easier. If your cooker is made of one piece, though, check on its immersibility. *Most of the slow cookers sold with detachable controls are not immersible and are so marked on the bottom. You should refer to the instruction-recipe booklet provided with each model to determine which parts are immersible. If in doubt, write to the manufacturer, giving the model number, and asking for specific instructions.*

Crockery pot slow cookers are available in various shapes and sizes. Capacity ranges from 2½ to 8 quarts. Most pots are round; some models are oval. Choose the design that most appeals to you. Slow cookers do *not* speedily regain heat and moisture that is lost when the cover is removed during cooking. So if you are one of those cooks who just must peek at what's cooking, be sure to select a pot with a see-through glass or plastic cover.

Different models of slow cookers have different heating controls. Some of the cookers have heating control panels that are permanently attached to the appliance. On most slow cookers, there are three settings on the heating controls—off, low, high. The low temperature is hot enough to destroy harmful bacteria in food. The high setting is about 300°F. Some crockery pots have heating controls that enable temperatures to go as high as 500°F. This permits conventional roasting, deep-fat frying, frying, and browning, but these "slow-fast" cookers will be far more costly to operate and use much more electricity than those with lower temperatures only.

Some crockery pots offer a control dial with an "automatic shift" position. After an initial period of cooking with heat, the temperature is automatically lowered. This helps quicken the cooking process and allows you to be away from the kitchen the whole cooking time.

The heating element of the crockery pot may be found either in its walls, or on an electric plate that comes with the appliance. If the cooker has an enclosed heating element, then its wires may be wrapped around the sides or along the bottom. Some cooks suggest that with side wiring, the heat is distributed more evenly and there is less chance of scorching, even though this is a remote possibility.

When selecting a crockery pot slow cooker, you want to consider these eight points:

1. The handles and legs should be heat resistant. The handles should be large enough so that the cookpot can be moved easily and safely, *especially when hot.*

2. The cover should be heat resistant, easy to remove, and see-through if you like to watch your food cooking.

3.the controls should be clearly marked and easy to work.

4. The temperatures should be explained on the panel or in an accompanying instruction booklet or leaflet.

5. The crockery pot should have an "off" position. Otherwise, you'll have to unplug it in order to turn it off.

6. The crockery pot should bear the seal of the Underwriters Laboratories. When you see the UL seal on the package, product, or instruction book, it tells you that the item meets the safety standards of the Underwriters Laboratories.

7. Your guarantee should tell you which parts of your crockery pot are covered and for how long a period. It should also tell you which parts are *not* guaranteed. Furthermore, the guarantee should tell you if your

crockery pot can be serviced locally while under this assurance; or must it be shipped, at your expense, to a special service center for repair?

8. If the crockery pot offers browning, frying, and faster-cooking features, ask yourself if you really need them. Such additional features use much more electricity. If you need them, prepare to pay a bit more for their use.

Summing up, you may ask, "Why cook with a crockery pot?" Here are the basic reasons:

1. It gives you freedom to plan your day without being tied down to your kitchen. No stirring, basting, or turning meats over a hot stove. Just prepare your recipe in the crockery pot and then enjoy your new-found leisure.

2. The crockery pot is safe. There is little or no chance of scorching.

3. The crockery pot is a money saver. An average high temperature setting uses about 140 watts, an average low setting only 70 watts of electricity. At a four cents per kilowatt-hour rate, you can cook the entire day on a low setting for about three cents. Isn't this a wonderful bargain?

4. The crockery pot is the dream of any homemaker who wants leisure time but good meals, too. This slow cooker gives food an improved flavor, and helps it retain vitamins and minerals that drain away in ordinary cooking. It also lets you use inexpensive cuts of meat.

Your crockery pot gives you a tasty, healthful, and convenient way of feeding your family.

Just taste the results...and enjoy!

Chapter Two
How To Use And Care For Your Crockery Pot

THERE'S A new arrival at your home. You want to know how to give it the best of tender, loving care. The new arrival is your crockery pot, and you will be thrilled, indeed, when you discover that it brings old-fashioned flavor into our jet age. So treat the new arrival with care and it will reward you with delicious foods and a minimum of fuss and bother.

BEFORE USING THE FIRST TIME

Wash pot and cover in hot, soapy water, using a sponge or dishcloth to remove any manufacturing oils. Rinse thoroughly and dry. *Caution: Do not immerse electric base in water!* You can "condition" or "season" the cooking surface by rubbing lightly with cooking oil or shortening. *Important:*

11

Remove control before cleaning the unit. The heat control unit should never be immersed in liquids!

HOW TO USE YOUR CROCKERY POT

Here are the basic guidelines: First, place your crockery pot on a flat, level surface. Make sure it is positioned so it cannot be accidentally moved, touched, or tipped over by you, your guests, or children. The cord should be placed so that it cannot be touched or become tangled, and is not in contact with the pot.

Now, follow these simple instructions:

1. Attach cord to electric base or insert control into the pot. Put food into the pot and place pot on base. If the crockery pot is to be used on a table which does not have a protective surface, it must be placed on a metal hot pad. Do *not* use a cloth mat or a pot holder; these may block free air circulation under appliance. The crockery pot may be placed directly on a table or counter which has a heat-resistant surface.

2. Plug cord into *110-120 volt AC electric outlet.* Be sure dial is set at OFF. If an extension cord is needed, use one rated at no fewer than 15 amps, and be sure that your manufacturer approves the use of one.

3. Turn dial to desired setting. Unit will heat within five minutes. If food requires 9 to 15 hours of cooking time, appliance may remain plugged in overnight.

NOTE: The electric base is designed for very slow simmer-cooking of foods and liquids. It will *not* bring liquids to a boil. For example, it will take about two hours for a quart of cold tap water to heat to 160°F.

4. Time and temperatures are approximate. They will vary according to the size and quantity of food being prepared. Food taken directly from a refrigerator will take longer to cook than foods already at room temperature. A small quantity may require a lower temperature setting.

5. Use smooth-edged utensils, such as spoons, tongs, or spatulas to prevent marring of the cooking surface. Do not use sharp-edged cooking tools such as knives, metal potato mashers, electric beaters, rotary beaters, etc. Scratching may occur. Very light scratches, however, will not affect a no-stick cooking surface.

6. At the end of cooking time, remove plug from the wall outlet. Let the electric base cool, then detach the cord. Allow the crockery pot to cool before grasping the heat control housing for removal.

HOW TO CARE FOR AND CLEAN YOUR CROCKERY POT

1. DO *NOT* IMMERSE THE ELECTRIC BASE IN WATER. After unplugging cord from wall outlet, wipe the chrome-plated base with a damp cloth.

2. Let pot cool completely before washing. Clean the pot and cover in hot, soapy water with a sponge, dishcloth, or nylon pad. A NONABRASIVE CLEANER MAY BE USED IF NECESSARY ON THE PORCELAIN FINISH (inside and outside of pot) and on the stainless steel rims. Apply with a damp cloth or sponge, using a circular motion. *Do Not* use a metal scouring pad or harsh scouring powder on the porcelain finish. After washing, rinse pot thoroughly. If detergent is not entirely rinsed off stained areas will appear when the pot is reheated.

3. The nonglazed areas on the bottom of the pot and inside of the cover will absorb water when being washed. This may cause spots. Therefore, before storing, let pot and cover stand inverted for a period of time, until completely dry.

4. Stains are easy to remove. If stubborn stains appear on the cooking surface, use a commercial no-stick, no-scour surface cleaner. Reseason surface after cleaning. Occasionally, a white mineral film may form on the porcelain finish. To remove, simply wip surface with vinegar, lemon juice, or a solution of cream of tartar and warm water. Reseason to insure the non-stick property of the surface. Do *not* use steel wool, metal scouring pads, or abrasives on the cooking surface or outer porcelain finish.

Should the porcelain finish become discolored, scrub *lightly* with a plastic sponge or nylon scouring pad and a thin paste of chlorinated cleanser and water. Then wash thoroughly with warm, soapy water, rinse and dry.

If stains occur on the aluminum bottom of pot, use a commercial cleaner for baked-on grease. Do *not* get this cleaning material on the no-stick cooking or outside porcelain surface, as it may harm the finish. A metal soap pad or aluminum cleaner may also be used to keep an aluminum bottom free of stains.

HOW TO STORE AND HANDLE WITH CARE

When storing crockery pot, take care to prevent scratching or marring the porcelain finish. Do *not* hit pot against hard surfaces. Do *not* use sharp kitchen tools in it, as scratching can occur, just as it can on a plain metal surface. Minor scratching or marring will affect only the appearance of the porcelain finish. It will not harm food cooking in the pot.

TIPS FOR SAFE USE OF YOUR CROCKERY POT

Let's have a quick look at safety tips for your pot:

1. Do *not* immerse electric base in water.

2. Always use cord supplied with your appliance. A short cord is provided to reduce hazards resulting from entanglement with a long one.

Longer cords and extension cords are available and may be used if the electrical rating is equal to or greater than the rating of the appliance, and if care is taken to arrange the cord so that it will not drape over the countertop or tabletop where it can be pulled on by children or tripped over accidentally.

3. Always attach cord to appliance *First*, then plug into 110-120 volt AC electrical outlet. At end of cooking or serving time, remove plug from wall outlet. Let electric base cool before detaching cord.

4. Make certain appliance is placed on a flat, moisture-free surface. Do *not* handle electric base with wet hands.

5. Do *not* use the pot in an oven. Do *not* use over a campfire.

6. Do *not* cook foods directly on the base; they must be prepared in the pot or other serving utensil.

7. When using a serving utensil other than the pot on an electric base, make certain that it is made of heatproof *glass* or *metal.* Do *not* use plastic serving utensils on the base.

8. Do *not* move or carry appliance when hot.

9. Do *not* place the crockery pot on an electric or gas range heating unit, under an oven broiler, or over an open flame. The direct heat will cause the pot to crack.

With this kind of care, your crockery pot will remain beautiful and your food will become more delicious with every meal you prepare.

HELPFUL HINTS FOR GETTING THE MOST FROM YOUR CROCKERY POT

*If your crockery pot has a glass cover, it gets hot during cookin, so use a hot pad when lifting it.

*Always attach cord to your pot before plugging into wall outlet. *Always* unplug from the outlet before detaching the cord from your crockery pot.

*Unplug your crockery pot when not in use. You may detach the cord and coil it loosely for storage inside the pot.

*Always keep your crockery pot on a dry, level surface, away from water, and always work with dry hands.

*Let your crockery pot cool completely before washing.

*Do *not* immerse your crockery pot in water.

*To clean the inside, remove food and let pot cool. Fill with hot sudsy water and swish clean with dish cloth. Use plastic or nonmetal scrubber to remove any stubborn spots. Do *not* use scouring powders or metal pads.

*To clean the outside, wipe with a damp cloth, then polish dry with a soft cloth. Wipe unplugged cord with damp cloth to keep it clean.

*Wash a heatproof glass cover (if you have it) as you do the inside of the crockery pot. Or wash in dishpan or dishwasher just as you would other heatproof glass.

*Do *not* pour cold water or liquids into a hot crockery pot. Do NOT put hot glass cover in cold water. *Sudden changes in temperature can crack glass.* Always let your crockery pot cool before cleaning.

*Roasts or large pieces of meat usually go into your crockery pot first. Arrange vegetables around roast.

*Alternate layers of smaller-than-roast-sized pieces of meat and vegetables in your crockery pot. Unless cooking without liquid, add enough liquid to cover vegetables.

*Use any liquid you like for cooking: water, tomato juice, tomato sauce, fruit juice, chicken or beef broth, wine, or whatever the recipe suggests. Do *not* use milk unless the recipe tells you to do so.

*Do *not* fill your crockery pot too full! One inch down from the lower inside rim top is full enough.

*Great gravies come from your crockery pot juices. Blend flour or cornstarch with cold water in saucepan (1 tablespoon flour and 1 tablespoon water for each cup of juices). Add juices from the crockery pot and then cook and stir over medium heat until thickened.

*Slice, halve, or quarter larger vegetables before putting them into your crockery pot. Surprisingly, vegetables cook slower than meat in your appliance, so place vegetables around the sides of the pot, near the heating element..

*You can cook *without* liquid. For example, just drop franks, knockwurst, Polish sausage into your crockery pot; cover and cook 2 to 4 hours, depending on the thickness of the meat.

*Potatoes bake to perfection in your crockery pot. Scrub and dry baking potatoes and arrange in your crockery pot. Cover and let cook 4 to 6 hours for 6 to 8 medium-sized potatoes.

*Cooking bags can go into your crockery pot. Place food in the bag, tie as directed, place in the crockery pot, cover, and cook as directed. Clean-up is easy!

*Keep the lid on! Your crockery pot cooks best if undisturbed. Lifting the lid can lengthen cooking time. If you need to stir, do it during the last few hours of cooking.

Some foods do not benefit from slow cooking, so do *not* use any of the following unless the recipe directs: noodles, macaroni or rice, seafood (except clams), Chinese vegetables, puddings or sauces made with milk or cream.

*Your appliance is not designed to thaw solid blocks of frozen foods unless there is additional liquid added. You may put frozen foods (vegetables, for example) in your appliance *along with other liquids, but add 1 to 4 hours of cooking time at HIGH or 3 to 6 hours at LOW. It's simpler to thaw foods before* putting them into your appliance. TIP: Overnight in your refrigerator (not freezer) will thaw most items.

*Slow cooking usually requires more seasoning than other cooking methods. Taste before serving and correct seasoning to your own preference. Highly seasoned foods (corned or smoked meats) usually don't need additional seasoning.

*When cooking meats and vegetables together on the LOW setting, be sure to place vegetables on the bottom or where they will be kept moist.

*To keep vegetables extra-moist when roasting on LOW, and when they are not covered by the meat, wrap them in foil or use 1 cup of liquid instead of small amount called for in the recipe.

*When recipes call for cooking more than 10 hours on LOW, you may start on HIGH for the first hour to complete cooking in a shorter time.

*When serving, spoon or ladle contents from your crockery pot. Pouring hot liquid from the cooker might cause the outer edge of the stoneware liner to crack.

IMPORTANT

*The temperature within the crockery vessel will vary depending on the type of food being cooked. Since crockery cooking utilizes very low temperature it is important that all of the food inside the crockery vessel become hot enough to be cooked properly, thus avoiding possible food spoilage. *Be sure that you do not fill the crockery pot above the slanted part of the vessel wall; this will insure proper heat distribution.*

Best results are obtained if the temperatures are at least 180°F., but in general they should not exceed 205°F. unless you wish to speed the cooking.

Chapter Three
How To Prepare No-Fuss Meals With Modern Slow Cookers

YOU'RE BUSY! You're tired! You're lazy! Or a combination of all three. But more important, *you're hungry!* You want to sit down, either by yourself or with others, and enjoy a delicious hot meal. But you want none of the time and labor that really good cooking demands. With the use of your crockery pot, little advance planning will enable you to come home in the evening and enjoy a wholesome, old-fashioned meal, with almost no fuss and no bother.

In the morning, you put in the ingredients. Then set the dial for LOW. Forget it. Let it simmer for 8, 10, or 12 hours. There is *no* stirring, *no* peeking, *no* worry, *no* sticking. *Your crockery pot cooks all day while the cook's away.*

FACTS ABOUT MEAT AND NUTRITION

Two meals may consist of the same foods, but be totally different. One meal might be tender, tasty,and very nutritious while the other is tough, tasteless, and lacking in vitamins, minerals, and protein. The difference may be caused by the cooking temperature and method.

Slow, even, crockery pot cooking helps keep natural flavor and juices in, where you want then, because the pot's thicker construction allows even distribution of heat. Concentrated heat can scorch and burst food cells, driving out flavor and liquid.

Meat consultants and home economists agree:

1. You get better flavor from foods cooked at low temperature.
2. Foods cooked at low temperatures are more tender.
3. Meats cooked at low temperatures are juicier because less moisture evaporates.
4. You will save more money on your food budget by cooking meats at low temperature because there is much less weight loss, and because less expensive cuts of meat can be used.
5. The higher the temperature, the more electricity you use, so you save money when cooking at lower temperatures.

QUESTIONS AND ANSWERS ABOUT YOUR CROCKERY POT

"Does it matter how I cut up vegetables?"

When roasting, it might. Most vegetables should be cut in small pieces, or at least quartered and placed near sides or bottom of your crockery pot. Carrots should be peeled and put where they will be covered by liquid. (An unusual characteristic of the crockery pot is that meats generally cook faster than most vegetables.)

"What are the average cooking temperatures in the crockery pot?"

About 200°F. (just below boiling) on LOW and approximately 300°F. on HIGH. Because of the "wrap-around" heating system of some crockery pots, low temperature and long cooking periods cannot accurately be compared to an oven or skillet.

"Can I cook small portions in my crockery pot?"

Yes, but cooking times will vary. Because there is no direct heat at the bottom, always fill your crockery pot at least half full for proper cooking to conform to recommended times.

"Explain the LOW and HIGH temperature settings."

The LOW setting uses 70 watts of electricity. The HIGH setting uses 140 watts. Slow cooking is the "secret" of outstanding flavor, retention of natural nutrients, and carefree economy. One hour on HIGH is approximately equal to 2 to 2½ hours on LOW. Most of the time, LOW is the most favored setting, however, some recipes call for HIGH because of the nature of the food being prepared or to obtain the best consistency for that particular dish. HIGH also comes in handy to speed the cooking time.

If a recipe says to cook 10 to 12 hours on LOW and you want to eat at 7 or 8P.M., but can't start the crockery pot until noon, just turn to HIGH for about 2 hours, then to LOW for about 6 hours.

"Shouldn't I stir sometimes while cooking?"

It's never necessary to stir while cooking on LOW heat. You do not have to stir while cooking on HIGH, but some recipes do suggest stirring once in a while. While using HIGH for short periods, occasional stirring improves the distribution of flavors.

"How about making gravy?"

Make it right in your crockery pot. Retain all that delicious flavor! Add some minute tapioca to any recipe when you want a thick gravy. It will thicken as it cooks! Or you may remove foods from the pot, leaving the juices. Prepare a smooth paste of approximately ¼ cup floor or corn starch to 2 cup water. Pour mixture into liquid in your crockery pot and stir well. Turn to HIGH and when it comes to a boil (about 15 minutes) it is ready.

"What if I end up with too much liquid?"

Since the liquid content of meats and vegetables will vary, you may have a dash more liquid than desired. the excess can be reduced by removing the cover and setting your crockery pot on HIGH for about 45 minutes. Most recipes cooked on LOW will be juicier since the low heat prevents boiling away of flavorful liquids.

"Can I cook a roast without adding water?"

Yes — if cooked on LOW. You may want to use a small amount, though, because gravies are especially tasty. the more fat or "marbling" the meat has, the less liquid you need.

What if the food isn't done after 8 hours...when the recipe says '8 to 10 hours'?"

This can be caused by voltage variations, or altitude, or even extreme humidity. the slight fluctuations in power which occur everywhere do not have a noticeable effect on most appliances. They can slightly alter cooking times in the crockery pot, however. Allow plenty of time. Remember, it is practically impossible to overcook. you will learn through experience whether to use the shorter or longer time given.

"Can quick temperature changes harm my crockery pot?"

Yes. The cooking vessel within your crockery pot is usually stoneware. As with any fine ceramic, it will not withstand the shock of sudden temperature changes. So follow these rules:

•Do *not* put in frozen, or very cold, foods if the stoneware is hot to the touch.

•Do *not* attempt to wash your crockery pot right away after cooking, unless the water you pour in is *hot.*

Do *not* use your crockery pot as a container for storing foods in your refrigerator.

Can I put frozen foods into my crockery pot?"

Certainly—but increase the cooking time by two or three hours. Or start on HIGH for the first hour or hour and a half.

"What about frozen casseroles?"

Fine! And you can leave them in their aluminum wraps. Casseroles should be heated five to eight hours (depending on weight and shape). The crockery pot is ideal for this because slow, gentle heating does not dry out the foods. Again, better flavor!

"Must I brown meats first?"

Not unless there is considerable fat. Browning does cut down on the fat content. When meat is lean, there is no need to brown it first.

"Can you be more specific than 'cook 4 to 8 hours'?"

Basically, timing is not critical with your crockery pot. In four hours, the food would be "done." But in four more hours, it would be done a little more and be more tender. That same recipe could cook for 10 hours, yet still not be overcooked! The deciding factor is individual preference. Ask yourself how well cooked you want it. Or, you might be away from home for 8 to 10 hours and want your crockery pot to keep cooking during this period.

"Do all these hints apply to a standard 2-quart size crockery pot?"

Yes, but most of the recipes could be reduced. A 3- to 4- pound roast or a 3-pound disjointed chicken will fit very nicely in a 2-quart size crockery pot. Amounts of vegetables may be reduced.

"How much spice should I use?"

Generally, a modest amount of spice is helpful. Use whole spices in your crockery pot for best flavor. Ground spices may lose flavor during cooking.

"Should I fill the pot to the top?"

No! For best results, your crockery pot should be at least half-filled, but in no case should the pot be filled higher than 1 inch from the top.

What shall I do when cooking small amounts of food with little moisture?"

Place a light covering of aluminum foil on top of food to retain moisture. The use of foil is also recommended when roasting and the vegetables are not covered by the meat. Just wrap vegetables in foil and place on top of meat.

GUIDE FOR ADAPTING RECIPES TO CROCKERY POT COOKERY

This handy guide is designed to help you adapt recipes to your crockery pot—your own favorites and prized recipes collected from friends, food companies, or newspapers and magazines. Become acquainted with this guide. It will save you preparation time, dirty dishes, and guesswork.

In most cases, all ingredients can go into your crockery pot in the beginning and can cook all day. Many preparatory steps are unnecessary when using the crockery pot. For example, you need never brown or saute vegetables. If you feel unsure about a step, go ahead and follow the method given in the original recipe.

Here are a few hints to remember:

*Allow sufficient cooking time on LOW setting.

*Do not add as much water as conventional recipes indicate. Remember liquids do not "boil away" as in conventional cooking. Usually, you'll have *more* liquid at the end of cooking instead of less.

*Cook with cover on—except to boil off liquids after cooking.

*It's "onestep" cooking: many steps in conventional recipes may be deleted. Simply add all ingredients to the crockery pot at one time (liquids last) and cook 8 to 10 hours. *Exception:* milk, sour cream, or cream should be added during the last hour.

When adapting recipes to the crockpot, keep these suggestions in mind:

Liquids: Use less in crockery pot cooking—usually about half the recommended amount. 1 cup liquid is enough for any recipe unless it contains rice or pasta.

Herbs and Spices: Leaf or whole herbs and spices are preferred, but their flavor power may increase, so use only half the recommended amount. If you use ground herbs and spices, add during last hour of cooking.

Beans: Instead of soaking beans overnight, cook them overnight on LOW with water and 1 teaspoon baking soda added. Or parboil (soaking or parboiling is specially important in hard-water areas to properly soften beans.

Drain and combine with other ingredients. Cook according to following Time Guide. Be sure beans are softened before you add to any sugar or tomato mixture.

Browning Meats: Seldom necessary—except to remove excess fat. Just wipe well and pat dry. Fats will not "bake off" in the crockery pot as in your oven. Pork, lamb, bacon, and other fatty meats should be browned and drained before adding to your crockery pot.

Precooking: Do not precook seafood or frozen vegetables; just rinse and drain thoroughly before adding to other ingredients. These foods cook quickly. Best to add during last hour of cooking.

Sauteing vegetables: Never necessary! Just stir in chopped or sliced vegetables with other ingredients. Only exception: eggplant should be par-boiled or sauteed to weaken its strong flavor.

Since vegetables develop their full flavor through crockery pot cooking, expect delicious results even when you reduce quantities. If a recipe calls for 2 pounds of sliced onions, for example, you may use only 1 pound. Sliced fresh mushrooms frozen peas, or corn should be added during last hour for better color.

Toppings: When a crisp topping of crumbs, bacon bits, tomato wedges, or grated cheese is called for, add just before serving.

Dumplings may be cooked in broth or gravy on HIGH. Drop by spoonfuls on simmering stew or liquid. Cook covered for about 30 minutes.

Biscuit, pie crust or instant mashed potato toppings require baking. Transfer to a baking dish and follow recipe.

Pasta and Rice: If a recipe calls for cooked noodles, macaroni, etc., cook *before* adding to a crockery pot. Don't overcook; boil until just slightly tender.

If cooked rice is called for, stir in with other ingredients. Add 1 cup extra liquid per cup of raw rice. Use long grain converted rice for best results in all-day cooking.

About quantities: The quantity of meat, poultry and vegetables may be reduced without affecting flavor.

Casserole recipes often suggest a specific size of baking dish. Most recipes will fit into andy size crockery pot. Recipes for a 4-quart Dutch oven will fit the 3½-quart and 4½-quart crockery pots. For the 6-quart Dutch oven, use half the recipe.

MORE HINTS AND TIPS

*Those popular roasting and cooking bags work well in your crockery pot. Simply fill with meat and vegetables and cook as directed in the recipe.

*Use your crockery pot to speed thawing. Simply set to HIGH, place foil-wrapped frozen foods inside, cover, and let heat 40 to 50 minutes.

*Keep leftovers in your crockery pot for a later snack. You'll be surprised how long they stay warm.

Time Guide:

IF RECIPE SAYS:	COOK IN CROCKERY POT:
15 to 30 minutes	1½ to 2½ hours on High OR 4 to 8 hours on Low*
35 to 45 minutes	3 to 4 hours on High OR 6 to 10 hours on Low*
50 minutes to 3 hours	4 to 6 hours on High OR 8 to 18 hours on Low*

HIGH: 300°F.   LOW: 190°F.

Most uncooked meat and vegetable combinations will require at least 8 hours on Low.

*Enjoy crockery pot cakes with packaged cake mixes. Just follow directions in Chapter Five.

*For even cooking of food, cut foods into similar sized pieces. Put meat in pot first, then layer vegetables on top of meat. Vegetables requiring the longest cooking time should be placed closest to meat.

*Always store dried beans in an air-tight container to prevent moisture loss. If beans become dehydrated from standing on a store or pantry shelf for too long a time, the cooking period must be greatly increased.

*Your crockery pot should never be filled higher than one inch from the top. You can use any kind of liquid for cooking—water, tomato juice, tomato sauce, fruit juices, chicken or beef broth, wine, canned tomatoes or whatever liquid is called for in your recipe.

*With all meats and other foods that are seasoned before cooking in your crockery pot, use a little more seasoning than usual. The long, slow cooking makes foods tender and juicy but requires more seasoning. With foods such as corned beef, or smoked meats that are already well flavored, it is not necessary to add more seasoning. Be prepared to taste each dish before serving and add more seasoning according to your personal taste.

And now...let's feast on Grandmother's kind of cooking with the modern crockery pot. *Bon appetit!*

Chapter Four
Beans

COOKING TIMES for dry beans will vary according to their age and type, growing locale, and water hardness. For baked beans and chili with beans, it will be necessary to simmer the dry beans in three times their volume of unsalted water for 30 minutes. Allow to stand, covered, for an hour and a half or until softened. Drain and add remaining ingredients. For most other types of recipes, cook pre-soaked beans in your pot on HIGH for 3 hours, then turn to LOW.

Simple Bean Cookery: Bring beans to a slow boil on your range in a saucepan containing 3 parts water to 1 part beans. Maintain slow boil for at least 30 minutes. Allow mixture to stand covered for a minimum of 1½ hours *or until softened.* Then drain and use in recipe. TIP: For best results, place a piece of aluminum foil over top of pot, then put the cover on. If you do not use the aluminum foil, stir occasionally.

Since cooking times vary, experience will teach you the best cooking times for your favorite bean recipes.

Boston Baked Beans

1 pound dry California white beans, soaked overnight in water to cover
⅓ cup molasses
2 heaping tablespoons brown sugar, or to taste

¼ pound salt pork, cubed
½ teaspoon dry mustard
Water, enough to cover beans in pot
3 tablespoons ketchup (optional)

Parboil beans in saucepan for about ½ hour, reserving liquid from boiling. Place all ingredients in pot, adding enough water to cover beans. Cover and cook on LOW for 8 to 10 hours. Serves 4.

Southern Style Black-Eyed Peas

1 pound dry black-eyed peas, soaked overnight in water to cover
4 cups water
2 teaspoons salt
¼ teaspoon pepper

1 large onion, chopped
2 stalks celery, chopped (optional)
½ pound salt pork, sliced (or 2 ham hocks, or 1 hog jowl)

Drain beans and place in pot. Add water and remaining ingredients. Cover and cook on HIGH 1 to 2 hours and then turn to LOW for 8 or 9 hours. Serve over fluffy hot rice and pass the corn bread! Serves 4 to 6.

NOTE: 3 packages frozen black-eyed peas may be substituted for dried peas. Use only 2 cups water.

Chili Con Carne

2 pounds ground chuck
1 cup red kidney beans with liquid
2 cups tomato wedges
4 strips bacon, diced

1 medium onion, chopped
1 medium clove garlic, crushed
2 tablespoons chili powder, or more to taste
Salt and pepper to taste

Fry bacon in pan until crisp. Drain, reserving bacon fat. Saute onions and garlic in pan, add ground meat and brown. Add all ingredients to pot. Cover. Cook on LOW for 8 to 10 hours. Season. Add more chili powder for stronger taste. Serves 4 to 6.

Mexican Red Beans

1 pound dry red beans (pink or kidney beans) soaked overnight in water to cover
4 cups cold water
1 large onion, coarsely chopped
1 pound of tomatoes

2 garlic cloves, minced
1 teaspoon crushed red pepper (or 2 teaspoons chili powder)
2 teaspoons salt
¼ pound salt pork or bacon, chopped

Put soaked and drained beans into pot. Add water and all remaining ingredients. Cover and cook on HIGH 2 hours, then turn to LOW for 8 hours. Serves 4 to 6.

New England Baked Beans

1½ pounds dry navy beans
9 cups water
1 medium onion, chopped
1 cup ketchup
1 cup brown sugar

1 additional cup water
2 teaspoons dry mustard
2 tablespoons dark molasses
1 tablespoon salt
¼ pound salt pork, ground or diced

Cook dry beans in water until softened. Drain and put into pot. Add all remaining ingredients; mix well. Cover and cook on LOW 10 to 12 hours. (HIGH: 4 to 6 hours, stirring occasionally.)

Favorite Chili

good

½ pound dry pinto or kidney beans
2 pounds of tomatoes
2 pounds coarsely ground chuck

2 medium onions, coarsely chopped
1 green pepper, coarsely chopped
2 cloves garlic, crushed

2 to 3 tablespoons chili	1 teaspoon pepper
1 ½ tablespoons salt	1 teaspoon cumin (optional)

Parboil dry beans until soft; drain well. Brown ground meat. Put all ingredients in pot in order listed. Stir once. Cover and cook on LOW for 10 to 12 hours. (HIGH: 5 to 6 hours.) Serves 4 to 6. NOTE: When using canned beans (2 1-pound cans), drain liquid.

Old-Fashioned Bean Soup

1 pound dry navy beans, soaked overnight in water to cover	1 teaspoon salt
	5 whole peppercorns or ½ teaspoon pepper
2 quarts water	½ cup chopped celery leaves
1 pound meaty ham bones or pieces of ham	1 medium onion, chopped
	1 bay leaf (optional)

Put all ingredients in pot. Cover and cook on LOW for 10 to 12 hours. (HIGH: 5 to 6 hours.) Serves 4 to 6.

Bean Pot Supper

2 pounds of pork and beans in tomato sauce	⅓ cup tomato juice
½ envelope dry onion soup mix	2 tablespoons honey

Combine all ingredients with ¼ cup water in pot. Cover and cook on HIGH for 4 to 5 hours, stirring occasionally. Serves 4 to 6.

Chapter Five
Breads-Cakes-Candies-Cereals

WHATEVER HAPPENED to the fragrance of good, old-fashioned breads or cakes being baked in the kitchen? Today, we see only mass produced products wrapped in plastic coverings in the supermarket. Remember the creamy, chewy caramels you used to love? Today, made in a factory and left in the display case for weeks or months, they are a far cry from the real old-fashioned confections.

Thanks to your crockery pot, you can now use the modern convenience ingredients for making a delicious and fragrant assortment of breads, cakes, candies, and cereals.

Steamed Nut Bread

1 egg	2½ cups flour, sifted
½ cup sugar	2 teaspoons salt
1 cup milk	1 cup chopped nuts

Beat egg and sugar until light. Add alternately milk and sifted dry ingredients. Add nuts. Turn dough into a greased mold or coffee can. Cover with foil and place in pot with 2½ cups water. Set on HIGH and cook for 2½ to 3 hours. After removing, allow to stand for 5 minutes before femoving from mold.

Boston Brown Bread

1 cup flour, sifted	1 cup stirred whole-wheat flour
1 teaspoon baking powder	1 cup chopped nuts (optional)
1 teaspoon soda	¾ cup dark molasses
1 teaspoon salt	2 cups buttermilk or sour milk
1 cup yellow cornmeal	1 cup raisins

Sift flour with baking powder, soda and salt. Stir in cornmeal and whole-wheat flour. Add remaining ingredients; beat well. Pour batter into greased and floured 3-pound coffee can. Pour 2 cups water into pot; place can inside. Place aluminum foil over top and fold down around edge of cooker. Cover and bake on HIGH for 4 to 5 hours. Remove and let cool 1 hour before unmolding. Slice and serve with wedges of cream cheese. Serves 4 to 6.

Caramel Nut Rolls

2 packages biscuits	1 cup honey
½ cup butter or margarine, melted	½ cup chopped nuts
	Cinnamon

Turn pot to HIGH while preparing rolls. Mix honey and nuts together. Dip each biscuit in melted butter, then honey and nuts. Place in well-greased 2-pound coffee can. Sprinkle each layer of biscuits with cinnamon. Bake according to instructions for *Basic Recipe* in CROCKERY POT CAKES listing in this chapter:

VARIATION: Yeast rolls (unbaked) may be substituted for refrigerator biscuits. Fill can with dipped rolls and let rise before baking. Bake as directed for 3 to 4 hours.

Pumpkin Tea Bread

1 cup oil	1½ teaspoons salt
1 cup honey	1 teaspoon cinnamon
1 cup molasses	1 teaspoon nutmeg
4 eggs, beaten	2 teaspoons soda
1 pound cooked pumpkin	⅔ cup chopped walnuts
3 cups whole grain flour, sifted	⅔ cup dates, cut up

Blend honey and molasses. Stir in beaten eggs, pumpkin. Sift dry ingredients together. Add. Stir in nuts and dates. Pour batter into greased and floured 3-pound coffee can. Place can in pot. Cover top of can with 4 to 6 paper towels. Place lid on top. Bake on HIGH for 3½ to 4½ hours. No fair peeking until last hour!

Crockery Pot Cakes

Basic Recipe: Pour mixed batter into greased and floured 2 or 3-pound coffee can or mold. (Fill no more than ⅔ full.) Place in pot, cover top of can or mold with 4 to 6 paper towels. Cover and cook on HIGH about 3½ hours. (Using 3-pound coffee can, cook on HIGH 4 to 5½ hours,) Crockery pot lid should not be tightly closed but slightly raised, to allow release of excess moisture. Add no water; *do not peek until last hour.*

Packaged Cake Mixes: Select a packaged cake mix (preferably a fruit, nut, or pound cake). Mix according to package directions. Pour into greased and floured 2 or 3-pound coffee can or mold. Bake as above.

"Fruit" Cake

2½ cups flour	1 teaspoon cinnamon
2½ cups sugar	½ teaspoon ground cloves
1½ teaspoons baking powder	4 to 5 raw carrots
½ teaspoon soda	1½ cups salad oil
¼ teaspoon salt	4 eggs
1 teaspoon nutmeg	¼ cup hot water

1 cup choppd nuts   1 cup raisins (optional)

Stir together flour, sugar, baking powder, soda, salt, and spices. Grate carrots to a fine consistency. (This may be done in a blender—blend 5 to 6 seconds.) You should have about 1½ cups of grated carrot. In large bowl, beat oil and eggs together. Add hot water and continue to beat. Stir in grated carrots. Add flour mixture, nuts, and raisins. Mix together thoroughly. Turn batter into greased and floured 3-pound coffee can, or 2½-quart mold. Place in pot. pot. Cover top of can or mold with 4 to 6 paper towels. Cover and cook on HIGH about 3½ hours. Pot lid should not be tightly closed, but slightly raised, to allow release of excess misture. Add no water. *Do not peek until last hour.*

Delicious Apple Cake

2 cups sugar

1 cup oil   1 teaspoon soda

2 eggs   1 teaspoon nutmeg

2 teaspoons vanilla   2 cups Delicious apples, finely

2 cups flour   chopped and not peeled

1 teaspoon salt   1 cup chopped black walnuts

Beat sugar, oil and eggs together well. Add vanilla. Sift flour, salt, soda, and nutmeg together. Add chopped apples to sugar mixture and beat well. Stir in flour mixture and nuts. Mix well. Pour batter into greased and floured 2-pound can. Bake as for *Basic Recipe* instructions under CROCKERY POT CAKES listing in this chapter.

"Steamed" Mincemeat Pudding

½ cup soft butter   ½ teaspoon cinnamon

1 cup sugar   ⅔ cup evaporated milk

2 eggs   1 teaspoon rum extract

1¾ cups flour, sifted   (optional)

2 teaspoons baking powder   1½ cups prepared mincemeat

1 teaspoon salt   Orange Honey Hard Sauce*

Cream butter and sugar until light. Add eggs, beating thoroughly after each. Sift dry ingredients and add alternately with milk, beating until smooth. Stir in mincemeat. Pour into greased 1½-quart mold or 2-pound coffee can. Cook as directed for Pumpkin Tea Bread in this chapter. Serve with *Orange Honey Hard Sauce.

Orange Honey Hard Sauce

½ cup soft butter or margarine   1 teaspoon grated orange rind
3 tablespoons honey   1½ cups confectioners' sugar

Beat ingredients together until light. To make pudding flame, top with Hard Sauce and add sugar cube saturated with lemon extract. When serving, light the cube.

Golden Lemon Pound Cake

1 package yellow cake mix,   4 eggs
    2-layer   ½ cup salad oil
1 package lemon jello   1 cup water

Beat all ingredients 2 minutes in large mixing bowl. Pour into greased and floured 3-pound coffee can. Place can in pot; cover top of can with 4 to 6 paper towels. Put lid on pot and cook on HIGH 3½ to 4 hours. Do not peek until last hour.

Blueberry Cake

2 eggs, separated   1½ cups flour, sifted
pinch of salt   1 teaspoon baking powder
1 cup sugar   ½ teaspoon nutmeg
½ cup shortening   (optional)
¼ teaspoon vanilla   ⅓ cup milk
                1½ cups fresh blueberries

Beat egg whites until stiff. Add about ¼ cup of the sugar to keep them stiff. Set aside. Cream shortening; add salt and vanilla. Add remaining sugar gradually. Add unbeaten egg yolks and beat until light and creamy. Add sifted dry ingredients alternately with the milk. Fold in beaten whites. Take a bit of the flour called for in recipe and shake berries in it to coat lightly. Fold in blueberries. Turn into well-greased and floured 2- or 3-pound coffee can. Bake as directed for Golden Lemon Pound Cake.

Caramel Candies

1 cup sugar
1 cup light brown sugar
1 cup white corn syrup
2 teaspoons vanilla

1 14-ounce can evaporated Milk
½ cup butter
1 cup chopped pecans

Mix all ingredients except vanilla and pecans in pot. Cook on HIGH, stirring occasionally, for 4 to 5 hours. Turn to LOW and remove cover; cook overnight or until mixture coats spoon. Add vanilla and chopped pecans. Pour on buttered cookie sheet (about ½ inch deep). Cool until completely cold. Cut with kitchen shears in size desired, and wrap each piece in food wrap. Serves 4 to 6.

It's certainly convenient to wake up to an "instant" breakfast. Right after the alarm clock goes off, you have to make yourself look presentable. You probably have to prepare breakfast for others. Time is of the essence. But you also want a nourishing breakfast that perks up sleepy appetites.

Go ahead and enjoy an extra half hour of snoozing after the alarm clock goes off. You can have a delicious breakfast waiting for you, piping hot, with the use of your crockery pot. Just make the simple preparations the night before. Now you can start the day off right with crockery pot breakfasts. You'll have lots of "go" for a new day of active living.

Cereals

Oatmeal Cracked Wheat Grits Cornmeal Mush
Follow package directions for quantity of water and salt per cup of cereal. Cover and cook on LOW 8 to 9 hours. Do not use quick-cooking varieties.

Perfect Rice Cooker

Rice   Salt
Water   Butter or margarine

Follow directions on rice package for proportion of rice to water. (Up to 4 cups of raw rice may be prepared in an average pot—makes 10 cups cooked.) Rub pot lightly with 1 tablespoon butter or margarine. Pour in rice, water, and salt. Cover and cook on HIGH for 1½ hours to 2½ hours, stirring occasionally.
NOTE: When turned off, pot will keep rice warm for serving for 2 to 3 hours!

Chapter Six
Casseroles

IT WAS a warm, touching scene, in days gone by, to find the woman of the house standing before the old potbellied stove, attending her scrumptious meals in the big, black kettle. Tough but flavorful meat, poultry or game turned hearty and tender from many hours of slow cooking, releasing mouthwatering aromas which drifted through the house with a teasing hint of good things to come.   The scene may have been charming, but today's homemaker cannot afford the time. With her crockery pot, she can enjoy casseroles without the tedious task of pot-watching.

The secret of electric casserole cooking is the long, slow, cooking method which utilizes moist heat at a temperature just below boiling. This method is valuable for tenderizing tough meats, poultry and vegetables since long cooking breaks down their fibers as quick cooking cannot do.

Meats are juicier because less moisture evaporates. Slow cooking in the tightly covered crockery pot prevents many important vitamins and minerals from boiling away. It keeps meats and poultry from shrinking. Vegetables stay intact but cook through.

By serving directly from the pot, meals stay piping hot for hours. Even cleaning up is quick with soap suds and a cloth. With your crockery pot, the food goes in and the cook goes out! Wouldn't Grandma have loved that!

Macaroni and Cheese Casserole

3 to 4 cups cooked macaroni	2 tablespoons butter
2 cups evaporated milk	1 teaspoon salt
2 tablespoons onions, minced	½ teaspoon pepper
2 cups Cheddar cheese, cubed	½ teaspoon paprika

NOTE: For thicker sauce, add 1 beaten egg during first half hour of cooking.

Place all ingredients except macaroni in pot. Cover and cook on HIGH for 1 to 1½ hours, stirring occasionally. Add cooked, drained macaroni and cover, cooking on LOW for 3 to 5 hours. Serves 4 to 6.

Green Bean Casserole

2 pounds fresh green beans, washed and cut up	1 cup Cheddar cheese, grated
10½ ounces cream of mushroom soup, undiluted	1 can waterchestnuts, thinly sliced
1 pound French-fried onion rings	Slivered almonds (optional)
	Salt and pepper to taste
	½ cup water

Spread in layers as listed above, making about three layers. Save enough French-fried onion rings to crumble and sprinkle over top about 20 minutes before serving. Add ½ cup water and cook on HIGH for 7 to 10 hours. (LOW: 12 to 18 hours.) Serves 4 to 6.

NOTE: If using frozen green beans, use 4 packages cut-up green beans. Cook on HIGH 4 to 5 hours or on LOW 8 to 10 hours.

"One Pot" Dinner

½ to 1 pound ground beef
¾ pound bacon, cut in small pieces
1 cup onion, chopped
2 pounds pork and beans
1 pound kidney beans, drained

1 pound butter limas, drained
1 cup ketchup (optional)
¼ cup honey
3 tablespoons white vinegar
1 teaspoon salt
Dash of pepper

Brown ground beef in skillet; drain off fat and put beef in pot. Brown bacon and onions; drain off fat. Add bacon, onions and remaining ingredients to pot. Stir together well. Cover and cook on LOW 4 to 6 hours. Serves 4 to 6.

Beef and Egg Casserole

2 cups uncooked elbow macaroni
20 ounces cream of mushroom soup, undiluted
1 cup sliced cooked beef, shredded

1½ cups Cheddar cheese, cubed
1 tablespoon butter or margarine
4 hard-cooked eggs, diced
½ medium onion, chopped

2 cups evaporated milk

Combine all ingredients in pot. stir thoroughly. Cover and cook on LOW 5 to 7 hours. (HIGH: 3 hours.)

Cheese and Potato Casserole

2-pounds sliced potatoes
20 ounces Cheddar cheese soup

13 ounces evaporated milk
½ cup sliced onion rings
Salt and pepper

Combine frozen vegetables, soup, milk, and half the onion rings. Pour into greased pot. Add salt and pepper to taste. Cover and cook on LOW 8 to 9 hours. (HIGH: 4 hours) Sprinkle remaining onion rings over top before serving. Serves 4 to 6.
NOTE: Recipe may be cut in half, if desired. Cooking times are the same.

Tuna Noodle Casserole

2½ cups dry noodles
1 teaspoon salt
½ cup onions, finely chopped
8 ounces peas, with liquid
1 can tuna

10 ounces cream of mushroom
  soup, undiluted
½ can water
¼ cup almonds
½ cup shredded Swiss cheese
  (optional)

Put ingredients in pot in order listed. Cover and cook on HIGH 2 to 3 hours. Stir occasionally. (LOW: 6 to 8 hours.) Serves 4 to 6.

Apple-Ham Casserole

3 cups cooked ham, diced
2 tablespoons prepared
  mustard
2 apples, cored and sliced

2 tablespoons lemon juice
½ cup brown sugar
1 teaspoon grated orange rind
2 tablespoons flour

1 cup water

Put ham in pot and spread with mustard. Arrange apples over ham and sprinkle with lemon juice. Combine brown sugar, rind and flour with water and pour over contents. Cover and cook on LOW for 6 to 8 hours, stirring occasionally. Serves 4 to 6.

Veal Casserole

3 pounds veal, cut for stew
1 medium onion, chopped
½ cup slivered almonds

½ teaspoon rosemay
1 can cream of chicken
  soup,undiluted

Place all ingredients in pot. Cover and cook on LOW for 5 to 7 hours. If mixture appears somewhat dry, add a small amount of water and stir. Serves 4 to 6.

California Pilaf

2 pounds ground beef	1 small onion, chopped
2½ cups water	2½ teaspoons salt
8 ounces tomato sauce	¼ teaspoon pepper
1 green pepper, chopped	⅔ cup ripe olives, sliced
2 small garlic cloves, minced (optional)	1⅓ cups raw long grain rice

Brown ground beef in skillet; drain off fat. Place ground beef and all remaining ingredients in pot. Stir well. Cover and cook on LOW 5 to 6 hours. (HIGH: 3 hours.) Serves 4 to 6.

Green Rice Casserole

1⅓ cups evaporated milk	2 cups fresh parsley leaves, minced
½ cup cooking oil	
3 eggs	2 teaspoons salt
¼ small onion, minced	¼ teaspoon pepper
½ small carrot, minced (optional)	1 cup sharp cheese, shredded
	3 cups cooked long grain rice

In large bowl, beat milk, oil and eggs together until well combined. Add all remaining ingredients; mix well. Pour into greased pot. Cover and cook on highen set on LOW for 4 to 6 hours. Stir during first hour of cooking. Serves 4 to 6.

Corn 'N' Ham Casserole

¼ cup butter or margarine	¼ cup flour

½ small green pepper, chopped
½ teaspoon paprika
¾ teaspoon salt
¼ teaspoon pepper
⅛ teaspoon each: ground thyme and majoram
½ teaspoon dry mustard

2 cups milk
8 ounces cream-style corn
2 cups cooked potatoes, diced (optional)
1 medium onion, chopped
2 cups cooked ham, diced
1 cup sharp Cheddar cheese, shredded

Melt butter in saucepan; add green pepper and saute. Stir in flour and seasonings. Gradually stir in milk and cook until thick. Add to pot with all remaining ingredients; stir well. Cover and cook on LOW 6 to 8 hours. Serves 4 to 6.

Spinach Casserole

10 ounces chopped spinach, thawed and drained
2 cups cream-style cottage cheese
½ cup butter, cut into pieces

1½ cups mild cheddar cheese, cubed
3 eggs, beaten
¼ cup flour
1 teaspoon salt

Thoroughly combine all ingredients in mixing bowl. Pour into greased pot. Cover and cook on HIGH 1 hour, then turn to LOW for 4 to 5 hours. Serves 4 to 6.

Old World Sauerkraut Supper

3 strips bacon, cut into small pieces
1½ tablespoons flour
2 ounces sauerkraut
2 small apples, cubed
2 small potatoes, cubed

3 tablespoons brown sugar
1½ teaspoons caraway seeds
3 pounds Polish sausage, cut into pieces
½ cup water

Fry bacon until crisp; remove from skillet and set aside. Add flour to bacon drippings and blend well. Stir in sauerkraut; mix well. Place sauerkraut mixture and bacon pieces in pot. Add all other ingredients; stir together thoroughly. Cover and cook on LOW for 7 to 9 hours. (HIGH: 3 to 4 hours.) Serves 4 to 6.

Hamburger Casserole

1½ pounds lean ground beef
2 large potatoes, sliced
2 to 3 medium carrots, sliced
8 ounces peas, well drained

3 medium onions, sliced
2 stalks of celery, sliced
10½ ounces cream of mushroom soup, undiluted

Brown beef, lightly. Place layers of the vegetables, in the order given, in the pot. Season each layer with salt and pepper. Put the lightly browned ground beef on top of the celery. Mix the tomato soup with the water and pour into pot. Cover and set to LOW for 6 to 8 hours. (HIGH: 2 to 4 hours, stirring occasionally.) Serves 4 to 6.

No Peek Beef Casserole

2 pounds stew beef, cut into 1-inch pieces
1 envelope onion soup mix
10½ ounces cream of mushroom soup, undiluted

1 4-ounce can whole mushrooms
½ cup red wine or fruit juice

Combine all ingredients in pot. Stir together well. Cover and cook on LOW for 8 to 12 hours. (HIGH: 5 to 6 hours.) Serve over noodles or rice. Serves 4 to 6.

Chapter Seven
Cheeses And Fondues

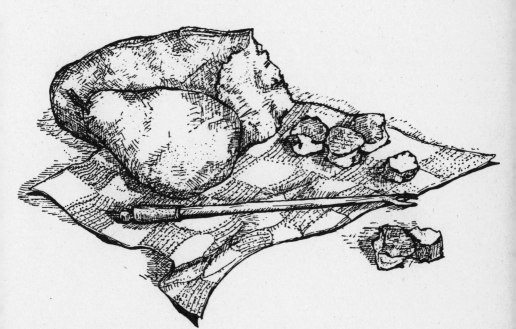

WHETHER IT is macaroni and cheese, a cooked cheese dessert, or a cheese dip, you want to get the best flavor from this dairy food.

Well, no need to count the minutes or the hours to prepare a tasty dairy meal. With your crockery pot, you need only measure in the ingredients and then let this slow cooker do the rest of the work...while you use your precious time as you want to. Your slow cooker will have your cheese meal waiting for you at the appointed time. The taste is superb!

Welsh Rarebit

| 2 | pounds sharp Cheddar cheese, shredded | 1 teaspoon salt |
| | | Cayenne pepper |

10 ounces tomato soup, undiluted

4 egg yolks, beaten

8 toast slices (or bread sticks or saltines)

Put all ingredients except egg yolks and toast or crackers into pot. Cover and cook on HIGH until cheese melts; stir well. Beat in egg yolks, using medium or low speed mixer; beat until smooth. Turn pot to LOW until serving time — 2 to 6 hours. Serve over toast slices or crackers, or as a hot dip with bread sticks. Serves 4 to 6.

Macaroni and Cheese

3 to 4 cups cooked macaroni
2 tablespoons onion, minced
1 egg, beaten (optional)
2 cups Cheddar cheese, cubed

2 tablespoons butter
Sauce Ingredients:
2 cups evaporated milk
½ teaspoon paprika
1 teaspoon salt

Put all sauce ingredients in pot. Stir well. Add other ingredients, cover and cook on HIGH 1 hour, stirring occasionally. Add cooked and drained macaroni. Cover and cook on LOW for 3 to 5 hours. Serves 4 to 6. NOTE: For thicker recipe, add 1 beaten egg to sauce mixture before adding cooked macaroni.

It's party time and that often calls for a fondue. This Swiss-cheese-dip party idea is more than just a lot of good fun; it's good taste and good nutrition, too. Usually, you add your favorite cheese and melting. But thanks to the use of a slow cooker, you can turn a fondue into a full meal!

That's right. You can add meat slices, vegetables, various herbs and spices, and let your slow cooker transform them into an exciting meal.

Hearty Fondue

1¾ cups milk
2 cups cream cheese,

2 teaspoons dry mustard
¼ cup chopped green onion

3 slices lean beef

French bread, cut into bitesize pieces

Heat milk in pot on HIGH. Add cream cheese. Stir until cheese is melted. Add mustard, onion and dried beef. Cook 5 minutes longer, then set on LOW for serving with bread pieces. Serves 4 to 6.

Dessert Fondue

1 cup carob powder
1½ cups honey
½ cup butter or margarine
⅛ teaspoon salt

3 tablespoons creme de cacao, orange-flavored liqueur, or rum
¼ cup milk or cream

Dessert fondue dippers (Angel cake, pound cake, marshmallows, apples or bananas, cut in bite size pieces)
Put all ingredients in pot. Stir together thoroughly. Cover and set on HIGH for 30 minutes. Stir well and set on LOW 2 to 6 hours. Serve with dippers. Serves 4 to 6.

Chili-Cheese Dip

1   pound lean ground beef
1   pound American cheese, cut
     in small pieces
½ teaspoon chili

8 to 10 ounces green chilies and tomatoes
2   teaspoons   Worcestershire sauce

Brown ground beef well and drain off excess grease. Put ground beef and all remaining ingredients in pot. Stir well. Cover and cook on HIGH for 1 hour, stirring until cheese is fully melted. Serve immediately or turn to LOW for serving up to 6 hours later. Serve with tortilla or corn chips. NOTE: For thicker dip, stir in a paste of 2 tablespoons flour and 3 tablespoons water.

Chapter Eight
Fruits

REMEMBER THE fresh-from-the-orchard aroma and tangy sweetness of homemade fruit desserts? While you can get just about every fruit in a can or jar, it just does not taste the same. But you feel lazy (rightfully so), and are not inclined to stir cooking fruits over a hot stove for hours and hours...especially in the summer, when many fresh fruits are available. Thanks to the electric slow cooker, you can enjoy the naturally sweet goodness of home-prepared fruit desserts without fuss or bother. It's a blending of the old-fashioned with the modern. And the taste...what joy!

Hot Fruit Compote

1 pound dried prunes   1⅓ cup dried apricots

1 ⅔ cups pineapple chunks, undrained

1 pound pitted dark sweet cherries

¼ cup dry white wine

2 cups water

Put all ingredients in pot. Cover and cook on LOW overnight or from 7 to 8 hours. (HIGH: 3 to 4 hours.) Serve warm. Serves 4 to 6.

Baked Apples

6 to 8 medium baking apples, washed and cored

2 tablespoons raisins

¼ cup sugar

1 teaspoon cinnamon

2 tablespoons butter

½ cup water

Mix raisins and sugar; fill center of apples. Sprinkle with cinnamon and dot with butter. Place in pot; add water. Cover and cook on LOW overnight or 8 hours. Serves 4 to 6.

Dried Fruits

Place dried fruit in pot. Add minimum water as directed on dried fruit package. Cover and cook on LOW overnight. Serve warm with sour cream and dash of nutmeg.

Chunk-Style Applesauce

8 to 10 large cooking apples, peeled, cored, and sliced or cut in chunks

½ cup water

1 teaspoon cinnamon

½ to 1 cup sugar

Put all ingredients into pot. Cover and cook on LOW overnight or 8 to 10 hours. Serve warm with or without cream. Serves 6 to 8.

Poached Pears in Red Wine

2 cups port or dry red wine

2 cups sugar

6 to 8 medium pears, ripe   4 thin strips lemon peel

Put wine and sugar in pot. Cover and cook on HIGH until sugar is dissolved. Peel pears, keeping whole and leaving stems on. Put into pot, turning to coat well. Add food coloring and lemon peel. Cover and cook on LOW 4 to 6 hours, turning occasionally to coat with wine mixture. Serve with wine poured over pears. Serves 4 to 6.

Chapter Nine
Hot Drinks

JUST MIX ahead and allow to steep...mm-m-m good! You want to have a steaming bowl of hot buttered rum, perhaps, waiting for your guests or family on a frosty autumn evening. Just set the dial on your crockery pot as the recipe directs, and let this favorite kitchen helper do most of the work.

When you make hot drinks in your crockery pot, you enjoy perfect serving temperature, better flavor. Most important, there is no last-minute rush; you can be with your guests to enjoy the good taste of a really well-prepared hot drink.

Hot Buttered Rum

2 cups brown sugar
½cup butter
Pinch of salt
3 sticks cinnamon
6 whole cloves

1 whole nutmeg or ½ teaspoon
nutmeg
2 quarts hot water
2 to 3 cups rum

Put all ingredients in pot. Stir well. Cover and cook on HIGH for 2 hours, then turn to LOW for 3 to 10 hours. Serve from pot in warm mugs. Serves 15 to 20.

Wassail

2 quarts apple juice or cider
1 pint cranberry juice
¾ cup sugar
1 teaspoon aromatic bitters
2 sticks cinnamon

1 teaspoon whole allspice
1 small orange, studded with
whole cloves
1 cup rum (optional)

Put all ingredients in pot. Cover and cook on High for 1 hour, then on LOW for 4 to 8 hours. Serve warm from pot. Makes about 12 ½-cup servings.

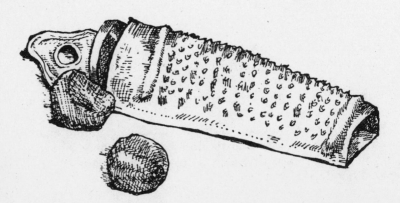

Chapter Ten
Meats

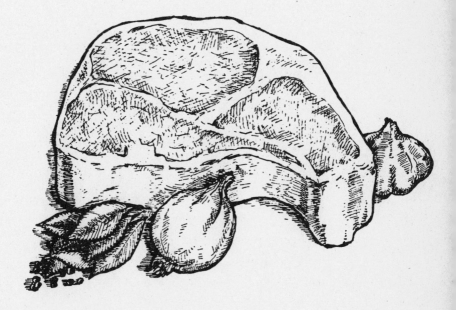

YOU WANT meats that are melt-in-your-mouth tender and have s-u-c-h flavor! It's yours, with the use of a slow cooker. Perfect every time—that's the reward of slow cooked meat dishes. Choose beef, lamb, veal or pork. Sprinkle with seasonings or any other flavors you choose. Your crockery pot helps retain the nutritional value of meats and softens their fibers.

You can enjoy meats that are succulent, juicy, and healthful, but demand a minimum of labor. Let your crockery pot cook all your meats for you, then just enjoy their good taste.

Boeuf a La Flamande
(Beer-Braised Beef)

4 pounds beef chuck, cut in 2-inch pieces
½ cup flour
2 tablespoons salt
2 teaspoons paprika
1 teaspoon pepper
10 to 12 whole small onions, peeled
4 strips bacon, cut in small pieces

1 pound fresh mushrooms, sliced
12 ounces of beer
1 teaspoon sugar
1 tablespoon vinegar
2 teaspoons dried thyme, crushed
1 bay leaf

Thoroughly coat beef cubes with flour, salt, paprika and pepper in large bowl or paper sack. Place onions, bacon and half of sliced mushrooms in pot. Add floured beef cubes and remaining half of mushrooms. Mix beer with sugar, vinegar, thyme and bay leaf. Pour into pot. Cover and cook on LOW for 8 to 10 hours. Serve over noodles or rice. Serves 4 to 6.

NOTE: May be thickened if desired. Make a smooth paste of 3 tablespoons flour mixed with ½ cup water. Pour into beef mixture. Turn to HIGH and allow to come to a simmer—about 10 minutes.

Bouillabaisse

½ cup olive oil
½ cup chopped onion
1 tablespoon garlic, chopped
½ cup chopped celery
1 pound tomatoes
8 ounces tomato sauce
2 teaspoons salt
1 tablespoon paprika
½ cup dry sherry or white wine
2 cups water

Pinch of dried basil
1 ½ pounds medium or large shrimp
3 sea bass or halibut steaks, cut in 1-inch pieces
crabmeat
4 medium lobster tails
1 pound clams or scallops (optional)

Put all ingredients *except* the seafoods (the first 11 ingredients) in pot.

Cover and cook on HIGH for 2 to 4 hours. Add seafoods: shrimp, halibut or bass, crabmeat, lobster, and clams or scallops (if desired). Cover and cook 3 to 4 hours on HIGH. Serves 4 to 6.

Boeuf Bourguignon
(Beef stew in wine)

6 strips bacon (or ¼ pound bacon) cut in ½-inch pieces

3 pounds beef rump or chuck, cut in 1 ½-inch cubes

1 large carrot, peeled and sliced

3 tablespoons flour

1 10 ounce can condensed beef broth, undiluted

1½ cups red wine

1 tablespoon tomato puree

2 cloves garlic, minced

½ to 1 teaspoon whole thyme

1 bay leaf, whole

½ pound white onions, peeled

1 pound fresh mushrooms, sliced

Cook bacon in large skillet until crisp. Remove from pan. Add beef cubes and brown well. Place browned beef cubes in pot. Brown carrot and onion. Season with 1 ½ teaspoons salt and ⅛ teaspoon pepper; stir in flour. Add broth, mix well and add to pot. Add cooked bacon, wine, tomato paste, garlic, thyme, bay leaf, and onions. Cover and cook on LOW 8 to 10 hours. Saute mushrooms in 2 tablespoons butter and add to pot about 1 hour before serving Serves 4 to 6.
NOTE: To thicken gravy, turn pot to HIGH. Cream ¼ cup flour and 2 tablespoons butter. Roll into pea-size balls and drop into pot. Bring to boil and let thicken.

Pot Au Feu

2 pounds boneless rump or chuck pot roast, cut into six pieces

1 pound pork tenderloin, or well-trimmed pork chops

2 to 3 chicken breasts halved, or thighs

½ pound Polish sausage, cut in serving pieces

3 carrots, scraped and cut in 3-inch pieces

2 onions, peeled, halved, and stuck with whole cloves

2 parsnips, scraped (optional)

2 stalks celery, cut in 2-inch pieces

6 peppercorns 1 bay leaf

½ teaspoon thyme

4 cloves garlic

1 10-ounce can beef bouillon

Alternate pieces of meat in pot; put sausage on top, and add vegetables on sides to fill up. Put herbs wrapped in cheesecloth or in tea strainer in the approximate center. Put in bouillon. Add more salt if desired. Cover and cook on LOW 12 to 18 hours.Serve with cooked carrots, leeks, turnips, onions, and potatoes. Serves 4 to 6.

Swedish Meat Balls

1½cups bread crumbs

1 cup milk or cream

1 pound ground chuck

¼ pound ground veal (optional)

¼ pound ground pork

2 eggs

1 medium onion, finely chopped

1 ¾ teaspoons salt

¾ teaspoon dill weed

¼ teaspoon allspice

⅛ teaspoon nutmeg

⅛ teaspoon cardamom (optional)

3 tablespoons butter or margarine

1 10½-ounce can beef broth

⅛ teaspoon pepper

½ cup light cream

Soak bread crumbs in milk or cream 5 minutes. Add ground meats, eggs, onion, 1 ½ teaspoons salt, ¼ teaspoon dill weed, allspice, nutmeg and cardamom. Mix well and refrigerate covered for 1 hour. Next, shape mixture into balls 1 inch in diameter and brown lightly in hot butter. Put meatballs in pot as they are browned, reserving pan dripping. (The browning step may be done in oven: place on rack or broiler pan and bake in 400°F. oven for 15 minutes.) Add beef broth, pepper, light cream, pan drippings, remaining ¼ teaspoon salt and ½ teaspoon dill weed to pot. Cover and cook on LOW for 4 to 6 hours. (HIGH: 1 ½ to 2 ½ hours.) Serves 4 to 6.

NOTE:Meatballs will have finer texture if meats are ground together twice.

Ham Steak In Port Wine

2 ham slices, each about ¾ inch thick

1 cup sweet cider

1 cup port wine (see note below)

½ cup maple syrup

¾ cup cranberries

¾ cup seedless grapes (or raisins)

6 slices pineapple (optional)

4 whole cloves

Juice of 1 orange

2 tablespoons cornstarch

Place ham slices in pot, rolling to fit, if necessary. Add remaining ingredients. Cover and cook on HIGH for 1 hour, then on LOW for 6 hours. To thicken gravy: set pot to HIGH and remove ham slices. Make a paste of 2 tablespoons cornstarch with 3 tablespoons water. Stir into pot. Cook on HIGH until thick. Serves 4 to 6.

Note: You will find this dish so delicious you can omit the port wine—if desired just cook in cider and syrup.

Sukiyaki

2 tablespoons salad oil

1 pound beef tenderloin, thinly sliced across grain

2 tablespoons sugar

½cup beef stock

⅓ cup soy sauce

2 cups green onions, cut diagonally

1 cup 1-inch celery slices, cut diagonally

1 cup thinly sliced mushrooms, drained

1 5-ounce can water chestnuts, thinly sliced

1 5-ounce can drained bamboo shoots

5 cups small spinach leaves

1 pound of bean sprouts

Skillet brown beef quickly in oil, turning frequently. Sprinkle meat with sugar. Cook celery in skillet until tender. Combine all ingredients in pot. Cover and cook on HIGH for 1 to 2 hours, or so that vegetables remain firm. Serve over rice. Serves 4 to 6.

Hungarian "Burned" Cabbage

1 medium head cabbage	½ cup dry red wine or beef stock
2 stalks celery	
1 stick butter	1 soup bouillion cube
2 pounds rump of beef, in one piece	Salt and pepper to taste
	2 cups broad noodles

Shred cabbage. Dice celery. Melt butter. Brown cabbage and celery over high heat, turning frequently. When brown, place in crockery pot. Place meat on a large piece of heavy duty foil, bending foil up around meat. Add wine or stock and onion soup mix. Wrap foil securely around meat and place on top of cabbage. Cover pot. Cook on LOW for 9 to 10 hours. Ten minutes before meat is done, boil noodles according to package directions. Drain and mix with cabbage. Serve meat sliced with the juices poured over the cabbage/noodle mixture. Serves 4 to 6.

Rump Steak Stew

1 pound whole rump steak	1 large can tomato puree
3 carrots, pared and cut in pieces	1 small can tomato paste
1 can white potatoes	1 teaspoon lemon juice
1 large scallion, chopped	1 teaspoon salt

Add all ingredients to pot. Cover and cook on LOW for 6 to 8 hours, until vegetables are tender. Serves 4 to 6.

Portuguese Pork With Chopped Clams

1½ pounds boneless shoulder of pork, fat removed, in large cubes	Salt and pepper to taste
	2 tablespoons peanut or vegetable oil

1 teaspoon paprika
2 bay leaves
½ teaspoon garlic powder

½ cup dry white wine
1 cup shelled clams

Sprinkle pork with salt and pepper. Heat oil in pan and brown pork quickly. Place remaining ingredients in pot with meat on top. Cover and cook on LOW for 7 to 9 hours. Serve over bread that has been sauteed in butter until golden brown. Serves 4 to 6.

Corned Beef And Cabbage

4 pounds corned beef
2½ cups water
3 to 4 carrots
2 onions, halved

3 potatoes, quartered
½ cabbage, cut in two
4 to 6 peppercorns

Soak corned beef in water overnight. Place in pot with water, chopped carrots, onion, peppercorns. Cover and cook on LOW for 8 hours. Add potatoes and cabbage and cook until tender. Serves 4 to 6.

Lamb With Eggplant

1½ pounds lamb, cubed
1 tablespoon salad oil
½ cup onion,chopped
1 pound tomatoes
1 clove garlic, minced
¼ teaspoon thyme

¼teaspoon basil
1 medium eggplant, peeled
  and cubed
¾ cup cooked rice
1 cup water

Brown lamb in oil in large skillet. Add onions and cook until pale and transparent—do not brown. Add remaining ingredients, except eggplant and rice, and simmer in skillet for 15 minutes. Put eggplant and rice in pot. Pour mixture from skillet over them. Cover and cook on LOW for 7 to 9 hours. Serves 4 to 6.

Magic Meat Loaf

1 egg, beaten
¼ cup milk
1½ teaspoons salt
2 slices bread, crumbed
1½ pounds ground chuck
½ small onion, chopped

2 tablespoons each: chopped
  green pepper and celery
4 to 6 potatoes, cut up
Ketchup
Green pepper rings

Mix eggs, milk, salt and bread crumbs; allow to soften. Thoroughly combine with ground chuck and chopped vegetables. Shape into loaf and place in pot. Top with ketchup and green pepper rings. Place potatoes at the sides of loaf. (If potatoes are peeled, coat with butter to keep from darkening.) Cover and set to HIGH for 1 hour, then turn to LOW for 8 to 9 hours. Serves 4 to 6.

Easy Turkey Jumble

1 pound, tomatoes
2¼ cups tomato juice
¼ cup salad oil
¼ cup onions,
  chopped
¼ cup green pepper, chopped
1 teaspoon salt
1 teaspoon garlic salt

Dash cayenne pepper
1¾ cups cooked rice
2 9-ounce package frozen
  artichoke hearts, thawed
3 cups cooked turkey, diced
¼ cup stuffed green olives,
  sliced

Combine all ingredients in pot. Cover and cook on LOW for 5 to 6 hours, stirring occasionally to distribute flavor. Serves 6.

Meatball Stew

1½ pounds ground beef
1½ teaspoons salt
⅛ teaspoon pepper
1 egg
1 tablespoon minced onion

½ cup soft bread or bread
  crumbs
1 tablespoon salad oil
3 tablespoons flour
1 pound tomatoes

1 cup water
½ teaspoon salt
2 tablespoons sugar
1 teaspoon crushed basil
3 medium potatoes, peeled and
  diced

4 small carrots, peeled and
  diced
1 onion, coarsely chopped
1 branch celery, sliced

Mix ground beef with salt, pepper, egg, onion, and bread. Form into balls and brown in skillet in hot oil. Remove meatballs from skillet. Pour off fat, except for 3 tablespoons. Blend in flour and stir in remaining ingredients. Add to pot. Cover and cook on LOW for 8 to 10 hours, or until vegetables are tender. Serves 4 to 6.

Boiled Tongue

1 beef tongue, fresh or smoked
2 tablespoons salt
1½ cups water

6 peppercorns
Juice of 2 lemons (or 2 onions,
  quartered)

Wash tongue thoroughly and place in pot. Add all ingredients. Cover and cook on LOW for 7 to 9 hours. Serves 4.

Beef Brisket Dinner

2 to 3 carrots, scraped
2 to 3 potatoes, pared
1 to 2 onions
3- to 4-pound fresh brisket, or
  pot roast

Salt and pepper to taste
½ to ¾ cup water
1 bay leaf

Place vegetables in bottom of pot. Add salt and pepper and meat. Pour in liquid. Add bay leaf. Cover and cook on HIGH for 5 to 6 hours or LOW for 10 to 12 hours. Serves 4 to 6.

Gourmet Dressing

8 ounces chicken livers, or 2 slices beef liver (optional)
1 large onion
2 cloves garlic, ground
2 stalks celery
1 green pepper
2 teaspoons salt
½ teaspoon pepper
2 to 3 bay leaves
1 pound ground beef
10 to 12 ounces fresh oysters
2 cups rice
4 cups water

Grind onion, garlic, celery, and green pepper with chicken or beef liver; add salt and pepper to taste. Mix in whole bay leaves; combine all with ground beef. Lightly oil skillet and bring to medium heat (not hot). Cook meat mixture slowly until meat is well cooked, stirring occasionally (it may be necessary to add a little water). Grind oysters and place in separate bowl. Place rice, water and 1 teaspoon salt in saucepan and bring to boil. Simmer covered, until water is boiled out and rice grains separate (about 30 minutes). Combine rice, oysters, and meat mixture thoroughly. Stuff bird. Place in pot. Cover and cook on HIGH 1 hour and then turn to LOW for 8 to 10 hours. Serves 4 to 6.

Beef Pot Roast

4 to 5 pound beef chuck, arm roast or rump roast
1 clove garlic
Salt and pepper
1 carrot, chopped
1 celery stalk, chopped
1 small onion, stuck with 3 cloves
½ cup dry red wine
¾ cup dairy sour cream mixed with 3 tablespoons flour

Rub beef roast with garlic; season with salt and pepper. Place roast in pot and add all remaining ingredients. Cover and cook on LOW 10 to 12 hours. Excellent served with hot buttered noodles. Serves 4 to 6.

"Smothered" Steak

1 ½ pounds chuck or round steak, cut in strips
⅓ cup flour
1 teaspoon salt
¼ teaspoon pepper
1 large onion, sliced
1 to 2 green peppers, sliced

1 pound tomatoes
4 ounces mushrooms
2 tablespoons molasses (optional)
3 tablespoons soy sauce
10 ounces green beans, French-style (optional)

Put steak strips, flour, salt and pepper in pot. Stir well to coat steak. Add all remaining ingredients. Cover and cook on HIGH 1 hour, then turn to LOW for 8 hours. (HIGH: 5 hours.) Serve with rice. Serves 4 to 6.

Sloppy Joes

3 pounds ground chuck or hamburger
2 onions, finely chopped
1 green pepper, seeded and chopped (optional)

8 ounces tomato sauce
1 8-ounce can water
2 packages sloppy Joe seasoning mix (optional)
Salt to taste

Brown ground meat in skillet; pour into colander and rinse well. Put into pot—add onions, green pepper, tomato sauce, optional seasoning, and water. Stir thoroughly. Salt to taste. Cover and cook on LOW 8 to 10 hours. (HIGH: 5 hours.) Serves 4 to 6.
NOTE: If mixture is too liquid, remove cover and set on HIGH for 30 or more minutes.

Corned Beef Hash

3 cups cooked corned beef, chopped
2 small onions, chopped

2 potatoes, chopped
2 eggs
1 teaspoon salt

½ teaspoon pepper

1 to 2 teaspoons prepared mustard

1 cup beef broth

Run first three ingredients through a food grinder. Mix well with all remaining ingredients. Press into a well greased pot. Cover and cook on LOW for 8 to 10 hours. Serves 4 to 6.

Old-Fashioned Beef Stew

1½ pounds chuck steak, cubed

1 tablespoon flour

3 medium potatoes, peeled and cubed

3 carrots, peeled

1 medium onion, halved

1 beef stock cube

Salt and pepper to taste

1½ cups water

Flour for thickening (optional)

Roll meat in flour and brown in pan. Combine remaining ingredients in pot, adding meat last. Cover and cook on LOW for 7 to 10 hours, or until vegetables are tender. For thicker gravy, add 2 tablespoons flour to 2 tablespoons cold water; add to mixture two hours before finish. Serves 4.

Osso Buco
(Potted Shanks)

3 tablespoons salad or cooking oil

4 veal shanks (or lamb shanks)

3 tablespoons flour

Salt and pepper to taste

1 clove garlic crushed

1 chicken stock

6 strips lemon rind

¼ cup white wine

2 tablespoons parsley

½ teaspoon majoram

¼ teaspoon whole or ground sage

½ teaspoon oregano

¼ teaspoon basil

1½ tablespoons tomato paste

2 carrots, finely diced

Heat oil. Roll shanks in flour, salt, pepper. Lightly brown in oil in skillet. Now put remaining ingredients into pot. Mix. Add shanks. Cover and cook on LOW for 8 to 10 hours until vegetables are tender. Serve with pasta and a garnish of fresh parsley. Serves 4 to 6.

Ground Beef Stroganoff

2 pounds ground beef
2 medium onions, chopped
2 cloves garlic, minced
½ cup sliced mushrooms, drained
2 ½ teaspoons salt

¼ teaspoon pepper
1 cup consomme or bouillon
3 tablespoons tomato paste
1½ cups sour cream mixed with 4 tablespoons flour

Brown ground beef in large skillet; add onions, garlic, and mushrooms. Saute until onion is golden brown. Put in pot with all remaining ingredients. Stir thoroughly. Cover and cook on LOW 6 to 8 hours. Serve over hot buttered noodles or rice. Serves 4 to 6.

"Texas" Hash

2 pounds ground chuck or beef
2 medium onions, chopped
2 green pepper, chopped

2 pounds tomatoes
1½ teaspoons chili powder
2½ teaspoons salt
1 cup long grain rice

Brown beef in skillet and drain off fat. Put all ingredients in pot. Stir thoroughly. Cover and cook on LOW 6 to 8 hours. (HIGH: 4 hours) Serves 4 to 6.

Beef Liver

Sliced beef liver may be prepared in the pot. Follow directions for SWISS STEAK in this chapter, using sliced liver instead of round steak. Dip liver slices in flour before adding to pot. Cover and cook on LOW for 6 to 8 hours.

Irish Stew

2 pounds boneless lamb shoulder or breast, cubed
2 teaspoons salt
¼ teaspoon pepper
2 cups water
1 small bay leaf, whole
2 medium carrots, peeled and cut in ½-inch slices

2 small onions, thinly sliced
3 to 4 medium potatoes, peeled and quartered (or 2 cans whole new potatoes)
10 ounces peas or mixed vegetables
¼ cup quick tapioca to thicken stew (optional)

Season cubed lamb with salt and pepper. Place in pot, alternating layers of meat, carrots, onions and potatoes. add remaining ingredients except peas; omit tapioca if you don't want gravy thickened. Cover and cook on HIGH for 1 hour, then turn to LOW 10 to 12 hours. Add peas during last 1 to 2 hours of cooking. Serves 4 to 6.

"Hickorysmoked" Brisket

Place 5-to 6-pound brisket in large piece of foil, or in cooking bag. Sprinkle generously with natural herbs and spices and ½ teaspoon each celery, onion, and garlic salt. Wrap well und put in pot. Cover and cook for 1 hour on HIGH, then turn to LOW for 8 to 9 hours. Serve warm with juices poured over each slice; refrigerate overnight, then slice thinly and cover with 1½ cups barbecue sauce and meat juices. Reheat for 4 to 6 hours on LOW. Serves 4 to 6.

Baked Ham In Foil

Wrap precooked ham in foil; place in pot. Cover and cook on HIGH for 1 hour, then turn to LOW for 6 to 8 hours. If desired, sprinkle ham with garlic powder before wrapping in foil.

Corned Beef And Cabbage

3 carrots, cut in 3-inch pieces
3 to 4 pounds corned beef brisket

2 to 3 medium onions, quartered
Cabbage, cut in small wedges
1 to 2 cups water

Put all ingredients in pot in order listed. Cover and set to LOW for 12 to 24 hours. (HIGH: 7 to 10 hours.) Push cabbage wedges down into liquid after 5 or 6 hours (LOW) or 2 to 3 hours (HIGH). Serves 4 to 6.
NOTE: Vegetables may be varied, or omitted for plain corned beef.
NOTE: To prepare more cabbage than pot will hold with large brisket, cook it separately in skillet. Remove 1 cup of broth from pot during last hour of cooking. Pour over cabbage wedges in skillet. Cover and cook slowly for 20 to 30 minutes.

Barbecued Ribs

3 to 4 pounds spareribs
Salt and pepper

1 onion
Garlic powder

Sprinkle ribs with salt and pepper. Place ribs in broiler pan under broiler for 30 minutes to brown and remove excess fat. Slice ribs into serving pieces and put in pot. Add onion and sprinkle with garlic powder. Cover and cook on LOW for 6 to 8 hours. (HIGH: 3 to 4 hours.) Serves 4 to 6.

Braised Short Ribs

3 pounds beef short ribs
Salt and pepper
Flour

2 medium onions, sliced
1 cup water

Roll short ribs in seasoned flour (about 1 cup flour, 1 teaspoon salt, and ½ teaspoon pepper). Brown well in large skillet. Put browned ribs in pot; add sliced onions and water. Cover and cook on LOW for 7 to 10 hours. (HIGH: 4 to 6 hours). Remove meat to platter and thicken gravy, if desired. Serves 4 to 6.

Barbecued Meats

Place seasoned and cut-up chicken, ham, or pork chops in pot. Pour a little barbecue sauce on each piece. Add no water. Cover and cook until done—about 8 hours on LOW.

NOTE: For added flavor, put cooked meat on heat-proof platter; pour remaining sauce and drippings over top. Place under broiler for 5 to 10 minutes.

Round Steak Casserole

2 pounds round steak, cut ½-inch thick

Garlic salt

Salt

Pepper

1 onion, thinly sliced

3 to 4 potatoes, peeled and quartered (optional)

1 pound French-style green beans,

10 ounces tomato soup, undiluted

1 pound whole, peeled tomatoes

Season round steak lightly with garlic salt, salt, and pepper. Cut into serving pieces and place in pot with sliced onion which has been separated into rings. Add potatoes and green beans. Top with tomato soup and tomatoes. Cover and cook on HIGH 1 hour, then turn to LOW for 8 hours. Remove cover during last half-hour if too liquid. Serves 4 to 6.

Lamb With Barley

1 clove garlic

1 large onion

2 carrots

Tops of two celery stalks

3 sprigs parsley

4 tablespoons olive oil

4 lambs' necks (about 3 pounds; have the butcher

crack the necks between the bones

Salt and Pepper to tast

1 ⅓ cups barley

1 cup beef stock

1 cup white wine

1 bay leaf

Dash thyme

Chop garlic, onion, carrots, celery and parsley very fine. Saute in 2 tablespoons of the olive oil in pan until onions are pale and transparent.

With a slotted spoon, remove vegetables to the pot. In the same pan, brown the lambs' necks, sprinkled with salt and pepper. While lamb is browning, heat the remaining oil in another skillet. Add uncooked barley and stir constantly until pale golden. Add lambs' necks and barley to the pot. Pour in bouillon and wine. Add bay leaf and thyme. Cover and cook on LOW for 9 to 10 hours. Serves 4.

Curried Beef

1 pound chuck steak, cut in 2-inch cubes
2 medium onions, chopped
3 tablespoons flour mixed with 3 tablespoons water
½ teaspoon salt
¼ teaspoon pepper
3 tablespoons oil

1 cup water
1 beef stock cube
1 tablespoon curry powder
½ teaspoon garlic salt, or 1 clove crushed garlic
½ teaspoon ginger
3 tablespoons mango chutney (optional)

Roll meat in flour, salt, and pepper. Brown in frypan with oil. Place in pot with all remaining ingredients. Cover and cook on LOW for 7 to 9 hours. Serve over rice, with or without mango chutney as garnish. Serves 3 to 4.

Stuffed Cabbage

¼ cup water
1 egg
1 teaspoon salt
Dash pepper
1 medium onion, finely chopped
1 pound ground beef
1 cup cooked rice
1 cabbage, using the large leaves

2 cups tomato puree
2 to 3 tablespoons brown sugar
1 teaspoon ginger
1 tablespoon lemon juice
8 to 10 finely ground whole wheat crackers, for thicker sauce
1 cup raisins

In a bowl, combine water, egg, spices, onion, beef, and rice; mix well. Immerse cabbage leaves in boiling water until limp. If you encounter difficulty in removing leaves, the entire cabbage may be placed in 1 inch of water and steamed at low heat on the stove. Remove heavy center vein of leaf by making a 1-to 2-inch triangular cut. Roll meat in cabbage leaves and place in pot. Combine remaining ingredients (and ginger snaps and raisins, if desired),and mix well. Pour sauce over rolled cabbage and cook on LOW for 8 to 10 hours. Serves 4 to 6.

Beef In Beer

2 pounds rump of beef, in one piece
¼cup peanut or vegetable oil
2 pounds yellow onions, sliced
Salt and pepper
3 medium cloves garlic, crushed

1 12 oz. can or bottle beer
1 tablespoon brown sugar
1 herb bouquet (parsley sprigs, a bay leaf and a bit of thyme in a little cheesecloth bag)
2 tablespoons cornstarch
2 tablespoons vinegar

Heat oil to smoking and brown beef quickly in pan. Place meat in pot. Add onions to the fat in the pan, reduce heat slightly, and cook until lightly browned. Add salt, pepper, garlic. Pour over meat. Pour beer over contents in pot. Stir in sugar. Tuck the herb bouquet down into the sauce. Cover pot and cook on LOW for 8 to 9 hours. Now, mix cornstarch with vinegar. Pour gravy from crockery into sauce pan, add cornstarch/vinegar mixture and cook on range until gravy thickens. remove meat from cooker. Slice, top with gravy, and serve with broad noodles. Serves 4 to 6.

Ham and Scalloped Potatoes

6 to 8 slices of ham
8 to 10 medium potatoes, peeled and thinly sliced
2 onions, peeled and thinly sliced
Salt and pepper to taste

1 cup grated natural cheese
10-ounces cream of celery or mushroom soup, undiluted
Paprika

Put half of ham, potatoes, and onions in pot. Sprinkle with salt and pepper, then grated cheese. Repeat with remaining half. Spoon soup over top. Sprinkle with paprika. Cover and cook on LOW 8 to 10 hours. (HIGH: 4 hours.) Serves 4 to 6.

Bourbon'n Beef Roast

4 potatoes, peeled and quartered	4- tolled roast
2 carrots, pared and cut into 3-inch pieces	1 bay leaf
	½ teaspoon basil
	4 ounces bourbon
2 stalks celery, cut inch lengths	¼ cup water

put all ingredients in pot. Cover and cook on LOW for 10 to 12 hours. (HIGH: 5 to 6 hours.) Serves 4 to 6.

Pepper Steak

1½ pounds steak, thinly sliced in strips	3 onions, thinly sliced
1 teaspoon butter	2 tablespoons soy sauce
1 clove garlic, crushed	1 teaspoon pepper
2 slices fresh ginger or ½ teaspoon ground ginger	1 cup beef bouillon
	3 green peppers, sliced in circles

Brown steak in pan with one teaspoon butter, garlic and ginger. Now add all the ingredients to pot, except green peppers. Cover and cook on LOW for 6 to 8 hours. Add green peppers and cook 1 more hour. Serve over rice. Serves 4 to 6.

Swiss Steak

2 pounds round or Swiss steak,   cut ¾-inch thick

1 large onion, thinly sliced

1 pound tomatoes

Salt and pepper to taste

Cut round steak into serving pieces; season with salt and pepper and place in pot with sliced onion. Pour tomatoes over all. Cover and set to HIGH for 1 hour, then turn to LOW for 8 to 10 hours. Serves 4 to 6.

'Lickin' Pork Chops

6 to 8 lean pork chops, 1 inch thick

½ cup flour

1 tablespoon salt

½ teaspoon garlic powder

2 tablespoons oil

10 ounces chicken with rice soup

Dredge pork chops in mixture of flour, salt, dry mustard, and garlic powder. Brown in oil in large skillet. Place browned pork chops in pot. Add can of soup. Cover and cook on LOW for 6 to 8 hours. (HIGH: 3½ hours.) Serves 4 to 6.

Cantonese Dinner

1½ pounds pork chops, ½-inch thick, cut into strips

2 tablespoons oil

1 large onion, sliced

1 small green pepper, cut into strips

4-ounces mushrooms, drained

¾ cup evaporated milk

8-ounces tomato sauce

3 tablespoons brown sugar

1½ tablespoons vinegar

1½ teaspoons salt

Brown pork strips in oil in skillet to remove excess fat. Drain on double paper towel. Place pork strips and all remaining ingredients into pot. Cover and cook on LOW for 6 to 8 hours. (HIGH: 4 hours.) Serve over hot fluffy rice. Serves 4 to 6.

Spicy Braised Ham

2- to 2½-pound smoked boneless pork shoulder butt

2 cups water
6 whole cloves
1 bay leaf

4 whole peppercorns
1 stalk celery, cut up
1 carrot, pared and sliced

Put all ingredients in pot. Cover and cook on LOW 6 to 8 hours. (HIGH: 3 to 4 hours.) Drain and serve. Serves 4 to 6.
VARIATION: For Spicy Ham Platter, slice cooked ham butt ½-inch thick and place in shallow . Make a glaze consisting of a 10-ounce jar of currant jelly, 3 tablespoons fresh horseradish, and ½ teaspoon prepared mustard. Heat and glaze and mix until smooth. Cover ham. Bake uncovered about 30 minutes.

Down South Barbecue

2 onions, sliced
4- to 5-pound pork roast, or
   fresh picnic ham

5 to 6 cloves
2 cups water

Put half onions in bottom of pot, then add meat and other ingredients with remaining onion on top. Cover and cook overnight or 8 to 12 hours on LOW. Now remove bone and fat from meat. Put meat back in pot. (Optional: Add 16-ounce bottle barbecuce and 1 large onion, chopped.) Cover and cook additional 3 to 5 hours on high stirring two or three times. (8 to 12 hours on LOW.) Serve on large buns. Serves 4 to 6.

✓ Hearty Beef Stew

2 pounds stew beef, cut in 1-
   inch cubes
5 carrots, cut in 1-inch pieces
1 large onion cut in chunks
3 stalks celery, sliced
1 large-size can tomatoes

½ cup quick-cooking tapioca
1 whole clove, or ½ teaspoon
   ground clove
2 bay leaves
Salt and pepper to taste

Trim all fat from meat. Put all ingredients in pot. Mix thoroughly. Cover and cook on LOW 12 hours. (HIGH: 5 to 6 hours.) Serves 4 to 6.

Stuffed Green Peppers

6 small green peppers, seeded
and tops removed
1 pound ground ham (approximately 3 cups)
⅓ cup raw rice
⅔ cup water

½ cup chopped onion
½ teaspoon salt
1¼ cups ketchup
½ cup water
4 carrots, peeled and cut in 3-
inch pieces

Wash green peppers; drain well. Salt cavity lightly. Combine in medium bowl: ground ham, rice, water, onion, salt and ¼ cup ketchup. Mix well. Stuff green peppers ⅔ full. Arrange stuffed peppers in pot (may be stacked) with carrot pieces to help support peppers. Pour in remaining ketchup and water. Cover and cook on LOW for 6 to 8 hours. (HIGH: 3 hours.)Serve in a bed of rice and pour tomato sauce over top. Serves 4 to 6.

Hungarian Goulash

2 pounds round steak, cut in
½-inch cubes
1 chopped onion
1 clove garlic, minced
2 tabelspoons flour
1 teaspoon salt
½ teaspoon pepper

1 tablespoon paprika
¼ teaspoon dried thyme,
crushed
1 bay leaf
1½ cups tomato wedges
1 cup sour cream

Put steak cubes, onion, garlic in pot. Stir in flour and mix to coat steak cubes. Add all remaining ingredients except sour cream. Stir well. Cover and cook on LOW for 7 to 10 hours. (HIGH: 5 to 6 hours stirring occasionally.) Add sour cream 30 minutes before serving, and stir in thoroughly. Serve over hot buttered noodles. Serves 4 to 6.

Brisket Dinner

5 pounds fresh brisket, well
trimmed

1 large onion, chopped
1 large carrot, chopped

2 teaspoons salt
1 bay leaf
½ teaspoon whole thyme
1 cup water

1 pound small boiling onions, peeled
6 medium-sized carrots, cut in strips about ¼-inch thick

Cut brisket in half or roll to fit into pot. Add chopped onion, chopped carrot, salt, bay leaf, thyme and water. Cover and cook on LOW for 10 to 12 hours. When meat is done, lift from pot gently, supporting underneath with spatula; keep warm. Add small onions and carrots to stock in pot. Cover and set on HIGH for 1 to 2 hours. Remove vegetables from broth with a slotted spoon and arrange around meat. Serves 4 to 6.

Spareribs, Cabbage 'n' Kraut

3 to 4 pounds lean pork spareribs, cut in serving pieces
Salt and pepper
1 small can sauerkraut
½ small head cabbage, thinly sliced

1 large onion, thinly sliced
1 apple, quartered, cored and sliced
1 teaspoon caraway seeds or dill weed
1 cup water
1 teaspoon salt

Sprinkle spareribs with salt and pepper. Brown spareribs for 30 minutes in heavy skillet or broiler pan. Put alternate layers of spareribs, sauerkraut, cabbage, onion and apple in pot. Add caraway seeds or dill weed to water and pour over all. Cover and set to LOW for 6 to 8 hours. (HIGH: 4 to 5 hours. Stir several times during cooking.)
NOTE: May be prepared using all sauerkraut or all cabbage, if desired. Serves 4 to 6.

Pot-Roasted Pork

4- to 5- pound loin and pork roast
Salt and pepper
1 clove garlic sliced

2 medium onions, sliced
2 bay leaves
1 whole clove
1 cup hot water

2 tablespoons soy sauce

Rub pork roast with salt and pepper. Make tiny slits in meat and insert slivers of garlic. Place roast in broiler pan and broil 15 to 20 minutes to remove excess fat.

Put 1 sliced onion in bottom of pot. Add browned pork roast and remaining onion and other ingredients. Cover and cook 1 hour on HIGH, then turn to LOW and cook until done—about 10 hours. Serves 4 to 6.

NOTE: To thicken gravy, remove roast to serving platter. Blend 2 tablespoons cornstarch with 2 tablespoons cold water to form smooth paste. Set on HIGH and pour in paste. Stir well and let come to boil—about 15 minutes—until thickened.

Pot Roast of Beef

2 to 3 potatoes   3- to 4-pound brisket, rump
2 to 3 carrots   roast, or pot roast
1 to 2 onions   ½ cup water or beef consomme
                         Salt and pepper to taste

Put half of vegetables in bottom of crockery pot. Salt and pepper meat, then put in pot. Add remaining vegetables, liquid, and salt and pepper. Cover and cook on LOW for 10 to 12 hours. (HIGH: 5 to 6 hours.) Remove meat and vegetables with spatula. Serves 4 to 6.

Roast Beef Variations

German Style: Add 3 to 4 medium dill pickles and 1 teaspoon dill weed to basic pot roast recipe.

Italian Style: Add 8 ounces tomato sauce, 1 teaspoon oregano and 1 teaspoon basil to basic roast beef recipe.

French Style: Omit carrots and potatoes from pot roast recipe. Add 1 cup fresh sliced mushrooms (or 1 8-ounce can), 1 pound small peeled onions and 1 cup red wine.

Without Vegetables: Season roast with salt, pepper and any other favorite seasonings. Add no liquid. Cook as directed above for Pot Roast or Beef.

Beef Stew

3 carrots, cut up
3 potatoes, cut up
2 pounds beef chuck or stew meat, cut in 1½-inch cubes
1 cup water or beef stock
1 clove garlic

1 bay leaf
1 tablespoon salt
½ teaspoon pepper
1 teaspoon paprika
3 onions, quartered
1 stalk celery with tops, cut up

Put all ingredients in pot in order listed. Stir just enough to mix spices. Cover and set to LOW for 10 to 12 hours. (HIGH: 5 to 6 hours.) Serves 4 to 6.

Veal Scallopine

2 pounds veal cubes (shoulder or shank)
¾ cup flour mixed with 1 teaspoon salt and ¼ teaspoon pepper
¼ cup oil
½ cup sliced mushrooms,

2 small onions, thinly sliced
1½ teaspoons salt
1 teaspoon sugar
½ teaspoon whole oregano
1 small clove garlic, minced
2 cups tomato wedges

Roll veal cubes in seasoned flour and fry in hot oil until well browned. Put into pot. Add all remaining ingredients. Stir together well. Cover and cook on HIGH for 1 hour, then on LOW for 6 to 8 hours. Serve over rice or fettuccine. Serves 4 to 6.

Stuffed Beef Heart

1 beef heart (about 3 pounds, split lengthwise)
1 clove garlic, minced
½ cup oil and vinegar salad dressing

1 cup beef broth
10 slices bacon, diced
1 medium onion, finely chopped
½ pound mushrooms, sliced

Fry bacon, onion and mushrooms in large skillet until onion is soft; drain. Trim fat and remove tubes from heart; wash well in salt water; pat dry. Fill heart with Mushroom Stuffing. Skewer or sew with string to fasten. Place in pot. Add garlic clove, salad dressing, and beef broth. Cover and cook on HIGH for 1 hour, then on LOW for 7 to 9 hours. Thicken gravy before serving, if desired. Serves 4 to 6.

Tongue

1 beef tongue (fresh or smoked)	1 bay leaf
2 tablespoons salt	2 lemons, squeezed; *or* 2 onions, quartered
1½ cups water	6 peppercorns

Place washed tongue in pot. Add all remaining ingredients. Cover and cook on LOW overnight (or 7 to 9 hours). Serves 4 to 6.

Easy-Does-It Spaghetti

1 pound ground beef	4 ounces dry spaghetti (1½ cups), broken in 4- to 5-inch pieces)
1 tablespoon instant minced onion	
1½ teaspoons salt	1 cup tomato puree
½ teaspoon garlic powder	½ cup mushrooms
¼ teaspoon each: mace, allspice and pepper	3 cups tomato juice

Brown ground beef well in skillet and place in pot. Add all remaining ingredients; stir well. Cover and cook on LOW for 6 to 7 hours. (HIGH: 3½ hours.)

Meatballs in Barbecue Sauce

SAUCE: Prepare first and put in pot to simmer while preparing meatballs.

½ pound butter or margarine	½ cup water

1 cup vinegar

½ medium onion, chopped

1½ teaspoons sugar

1 teaspoon dry mustard

1 clove garlic, minced

Juice from ½ lemon

Turn pot to HIGH while preparing sauce. Put all ingredients in pot; stir together well. Leave simmering until meatballs are ready.

Meatballs:

2 pounds ground beef

2 teaspoons salt

1 small onion, finely chopped

1 cup soft bread crumbs

½ cup milk

Mix together all ingredients and form into 1-inch meatballs or small hamburger patties. Place on broiler rack and bake in 400°F. oven for 10 to 15 minutes. Put browned meatballs (or patties) into pot with sauce. Cover and cook on LOW 4 to 6 hours. Serves 4 to 6.

Chapter Eleven
Poultry

YOU CAN "roast" a whole chicken in your crockery pot. Brush a roasting chicken inside and out with oil, then sprinkle inside and out with salt and pepper, perhaps a little rosemary and poultry seasoning , too. Place it into your pot, cover, and then let the slow cooker do all the work for you. You'll hardly ever need to add any liquid, either! This makes poultry taste the way it should...delicate, juicy, and fresh.

"Chicken In A Pot"

2 carrots, sliced	2 celery stalks with leaves, cut
2 onions, sliced	in 1-inch pieces

1 3-pound chicken, whole or cut up
2 teaspoons salt
½ teaspoon coarse black pepper

½ cup water, chicken broth, or white wine
½ to 1 teaspoon basil

Put half of carrots, onions and celery in bottom of pot. Add whole chicken or chicken pieces. Top with salt, pepper, liquid, and remaining half of vegetables. Sprinkle basil over top. Cover and cook until done on LOW for 7 to 10 hours. (HIGH: 2½ to 3½ hours, using 1 cup liquid) Remove chicken and vegetables with spatula. Serves 4 to 6.

Easy Company Chicken

2 cups cooked rice
1 whole chicken, fricassee style with gravy
9-ounces of artichoke hearts, drained

½ cup chopped fresh onions
1 lemon, thin sliced, seeds removed
1 cup white wine
Salt and pepper to taste

Combine all ingredients in pot. Cover and cook on HIGH for 3 to 4 hours. Serves 4.

Chicken Fricassee

2 to 3 double chicken breasts, or 1 chicken, cut up
¼ cup peanut or vegetable oil
1 carrot, diced
1 stalk celery, diced
1 medium onion, halved
Bay leaf
Pinch of rosemary

1½ cups hot chicken stock
1 teaspoon salt
1 egg yolk
¼ cup cream
2 tablespoons butter
2½ tablespoons flour
Salt and pepper to taste

Heat oil in frypan and brown chicken pieces, discard oil. Transfer to pot. Add carrot, celery, onion, bay leaf, rosemary, stock, and salt. Cover and cook on LOW for 8 to 10 hours, or until vegetables are tender (vegetables should be covered by liquid). Remove chicken from pot and keep warm. Strain stock. Beat egg yolk and cream together. Melt butter and stir in flour smoothly. Add stock to butter/flour mixture and cook in saucepan, stirring constantly until thickened. Add egg/cream mixture and stir to blend well. Season to taste. Pour over chicken pieces and vegetables. Serve with rice. Serves 4.

Sauteed Chicken Livers

2 pounds chicken livers
½ stick butter or margarine
½ teaspoon pepper
1 cup chicken bouillon
¼ cup dry white wine

1 teaspoon marjoram
2 tablespoons parsley
1 teaspoon oregano
2 to 3 cloves garlic, pressed

Brown chicken livers in butter. Add livers and all remaining ingredients to pot. Cover and cook on LOW for 4 to 6 hours. Serve over spaghetti or buttered noodles. Serves 4 to 6.

Coq Au Vin
(Chicken braised in wine)

6 bacon slices, diced
⅔ cup sliced green onions
1 2½-pound broiler-fryer, cut up (or 3 chicken breasts, halved; or 3 drumsticks and 3 thighs)
8 small white onions, peeled
½ pound whole mushrooms

1 clove garlic, crushed 1 teaspoon salt
¼ teaspoon pepper
½ teaspoon dried thyme leaves
8 small new potatoes, scrubbed
2 cups Burgundy wine
1 cup chicken broth
Chopped parsley

In large skillet, saute diced bacon and green onions until bacon is crisp. Remove and drain on paper towel. Add chicken pieces to skillet and brown well on all sides. Remove the chicken and set aside. Put peeled onions, mushrooms and garlic in pot. Add browned chicken pieces, bacon and green onions, salt, pepper, thyme, potatoes, Burgundy, and chicken broth. Cover and set to LOW for 6 to 8 hours. (HIGH: 3 to 4 hours.) Serves 4 to 6.

Chicken Parisienne

6 medium chicken breasts
Salt and pepper
Paprika
½ cup dry white wine or vermouth (optional)

10½-ounces cream of mushroom soup, undiluted
½ cup mushrooms,
1 cup dairy sour cream

Sprinkle chicken breasts lightly with salt, pepper and paprika. Place chicken breasts in pot. Mix white wine, soup, and mushrooms until well combined, stirring in sour cream NOW if you will be cooking on LOW. Pour over chicken breasts in pot. Sprinkle with more paprika. Cover and cook on LOW 6 to 8 hours. (HIGH:2½ to 3½ hours with sour cream added during last 30 minutes.) Serve chicken with rice or noodles, and pour sauce over all. Serves 4 to 6.

Chicken 'N' Noodles

3-to 4-pound stewing chicken or hen, cut up
4 cups chicken broth

5 to 6 cups noodles
Salt to taste

Prepare "Chicken In A Pot" recipe in this chapter, using 2 cups liquid. Remove chicken from broth. Turn pot to HIGH. When broth is hot and bubbling, add noodles. Stir well and cover. Cook 30 to 45 minutes, stirring occasionally. Serve with chicken. Serves 4 to 6.
NOTE: May be turned to LOW and held for serving up to 3 hours.

Chicken Livers

1 pound chicken livers
½ cup flour
1 teaspoon salt

¼ teaspoon pepper
3 slices bacon, diced
3 green onions with tops, chopped

1 cup chicken bouillon
10-ounces golden
   mushroom soup, undiluted

4 ounces sliced mushrooms
¼ cup dry white wine or
   sauterne

Cut chicken livers into bite-size pieces; toss in flour, salt, and pepper. Fry bacon pieces in large skillet; remove when brown. Add flour-coated chicken livers and green onion to bacon grease in skillet; saute until lightly browned. Remove from skillet. Pour chicken bouillon into skillet and stir into drippings. Pour into pot. Add browned bacon bits, livers, onion, and all remaining ingredients. Cover and cook on LOW for 4 to 6 hours. Serve over rice, toast, or buttered noodles. Serves 4 to 6.

Dressing

1 cup butter or margarine
2 cups onion, chopped
2 cups celery, chopped
¼ cup parsley sprigs
2 cups mushrooms
12 to 13 cups slightly dry bread
   cubes
1 teaspoon poultry seasoning
1½ teaspoons salt

1½ teaspoons sage
1 teaspoon dried thyme
½ teaspoon pepper
½ teaspoon marjoram (optional)
3½ to 4½ cups chicken broth
   or turkey broth and diced
   giblets
2 eggs, well beaten

Melt butter in skillet and saute onion, celery, parsley, and mushrooms. Pour over bread cubes in a very large mixing bowl. Add all seasonings and toss together well. Pour in enough broth to moisten; add beaten eggs and mix together well. Pack lightly into pot. Cover and set to HIGH for 45 minutes; then reduce to LOW to cook for 4 to 8 hours. Serves 4 to 6.
NOTE: If using a seasoned stuffing, omit herbs and salt.

Chicken Cacciatore

2 medium onions, thinly sliced
1 2½-to 3-pound broiler-fryer
   chicken, cut up

2 cloves garlic, minced
1½ cups tomato wedges
1 cup tomato juice

1 teaspoon salt
¼ teaspoon pepper
1 to 2 teaspoons oregano
  leaves, crushed
½ teaspoon basil, crushed

½ teaspoon celery seed (optional)
1 bay leaf
½ cup dry white wine

Place sliced onions in bottom of pot. Add chicken pieces, minced garlic, tomatoes, tomato sauce, salt, pepper, herbs and white wine. Cover and cook on LOW for 6 to 8 hours. (HIGH: 2½ to 4 hours.) Serve chicken pieces with sauce over hot buttered spaghetti or vermicelli. Serves 4 to 6.

Spanish Chicken

1 3- to 4- pound chicken, cut
  up
Salt, pepper, paprika to taste
Garlic powder (optional)

1 cup tomato puree
½ can beer (6 ounces)
1 small jar stuffed olives with
  liquid (¾ cup)

Season washed and cut up chicken with salt, pepper, paprika, and garlic powder, if desired. Place in pot. Mix tomato puree and beer together and pour over chicken. Add olives and cook on LOW 7 to 9 hours. Serve over rice or noodles. Serves 4 to 6.

Arroz Con Pollo

3 to 4 pounds chicken, cut up
Salt, pepper, paprika to taste
1 large onion, chopped
1 small green pepper, chopped
2 small garlic cloves, minced
1 small can pimento, diced
¼ to ½ teaspoon chili powder

2 bouillon cubes
¼ to ½ pound precooked pork
  sausages (or 1 cup diced
  ham)
14 ounces tomatoes
1 cup long grain rice
10-ounces peas

Season chicken pieces with salt, pepper, and paprika. Put all ingredients except rice and peas in pot. Cover and cook on LOW for 6 to 8 hours. (HIGH: 4 hours.) Turn to HIGH 1 to 2 hours before serving. Add rice and peas. Cover and continue cooking on HIGH until rice is tender. Stir occasionally. Serves 4 to 6.

Chicken Tetrazzini

2 to 3 cups diced, cooked chicken

2 cups chicken broth (or 2 bouillon cubes and 2 cups water)

1 small onion, finely chopped

¼ cup sauterne, white wine or milk

½ cup slivered almonds (optional)

2-ounces mushrooms, sliced

10-ounces cream of mushroom soup, undiluted

Parmesan cheese

Spaghetti

Put all ingredients except Parmesan cheese and spaghetti in pot. Cover and cook on HIGH 1 hour, then on LOW for 6 to 8 hours. Serve over buttered spaghetti and sprinkle generously with Parmesan cheese.
VARIATION: Place spaghetti in a large baking dish with sauce poured in the center; broil until lightly browned. Serves 4 to 6.

Chicken Tortillas

1 fryer, cooked and boned

10-ounces cream of chicken soup, undiluted

½ can (½ cup) tomatoes and chilies

2 tablespoons quick-cooking tapioca

6 to 8 tortillas, broken into pieces

1 medium onion, chopped

2 cups Cheddar cheese, grated

Cook chicken according to "Chicken In A Pot" recipe in this chapter. Cut chicken into bite-size pieces. Mix well with soup, tomatoes and chilies, and tapioca. Line bottom of pot with tortillas. Add ⅓ of chicken and soup mixture; sprinkle with onion and cheese. Repeat layers of tortillas, chicken soup mixture, onions, and cheese. Cover and cook on LOW 6 to 8 hours. (HIGH: 3 hours.) Serves 4 to 6.

Baked Chicken Hash

3 cups chopped cooked
chicken
2 small onions, chopped
2 small raw potatoes, chopped
3 carrots, chopped
2 eggs

1 teaspoon salt
3 tablespoons parsley, chopped
½ to 1 teaspoon poultry
seasoning or sage
1½ cups chicken gravy

Chop chicken, onions, potatoes, and carrots with food grinder. Mix well with all remaining ingredients. Pack into greased pot. Cover and cook on LOW for 8 to 10 hours. Serves 4 to 6.

Roast Chicken or Hen

1 3- to 4-pound roasting
chicken or hen
Salt and pepper

Parsley
Basil or tarragon (optional)
Butter

Thoroughly wash chicken and pat dry (patting dry assures good browning). Sprinkle cavity generously with salt, pepper, and parsley. Place in pot; dot chicken breast with butter. Sprinkle with parsley and basil or tarragon, if desired. Cover and cook on HIGH 1 hour, then turn to LOW for 8 to 10 hours. Serves 4 to 6.

Chapter Twelve
Relishes, Preserves, and Such

Do you remember? Long ago, a pot of jam or preserves used to simmer on the back of the stove. Now that old-fashioned flavor can be yours again, with your crockery pot.

Yes, occasional stirring is necessary on HIGH, but there is no worry about scorching. Cooking method and times will be similar to the Peach Butter recipe in this chapter. If a thicker preserve is desired, continue cooking overnight on LOW with the cover removed. No need to stir on the LOW setting. Use your crockery pot for preserves, jam, chutney, or fruit butter as well as most relishes and sauces.

Peach or Apricot Butter

5 pounds of peaches or
apricots
3 to 4 cups honey

2 teaspoons cinnamon
1 teaspoon cloves

Remove pits from peaches or appricots; puree fruits using blender or food strainer. Pour into pot. Add remaining ingredients. Cover and cook on HIGH 8 to 10 hours. Remove cover during half of cooking. Stir occasionally.
VARIATION: *Fresh Peach or Apricot Butter:* Wash, peel, pit and cook fresh fruit until soft. Add honey when cooked (using ½ to ¾ cup honey to each cup of fruit). Add spices and cook as directed in recipe above. Serves 4 to 6.

Chili Sauce

5 dried chili peppers,
3 pounds tomatoes wedges
1 medium onion, chopped
2 cloves garlic, minced
¼ cup olive oil
2 tablespoons parsley flakes

¼ cup honey
2 teaspoons salt
1 teaspoon fresh ground pep-
per
3 tablespoons red wine vinegar

Put all ingredients in pot. Cover and cook on LOW 12 to 18 hours. (HIGH: 5 to 6 hours.) Remove cover during last hour.
NOTE: Consistency is improved if half the sauce at a time is put in blender container and blended until smooth.

Hot Hollandaise Sauce
(How To Keep From Curdling, Too)

Prepare a double recipe of your favorite hollandaise or bearnaise sauce. Set aside. Set pot to HIGH for 15 minutes, then turn to LOW. Now pour sauce into pot; stir occasionally. Will keep perfect serving temperature for 2 to 6 hours. Sauce may be thinned with small amounts of water, or thickened by cooking on HIGH, uncovered, for a few minutes. Serves 4 to 6.

Chapter Thirteen
Rice

YOU WANT the solid taste of good, stick-to-your-ribs rice but modern convenience calls for the "instant" type of rice. Well, you can enjoy the solid taste of good rice, with little of the fuss required to cook the "old fashioned" variety.

Here are recipes that help you transform simple rice dishes into festive meals with the use of your crockery pot. You can feast on good, old-fashioned rice with little effort, using your slow cooker.

Old-Fashioned Rice Pudding

2½ cups cooked rice
1½ cups evaporated milk (or scalded milk)
2/3 cup brown or white sugar
3 tablespoons soft butter
2 teaspoons vanilla

½ to 1 teaspoon nutmeg   ½ to   cup raisins
3 eggs, beaten

Thoroughly combine rice with all remaining ingredients. Pour into lightly greased pot. Cover and cook on HIGH for 1 to 2 hours. (LOW: 4 to 6 hours.) Stir during first 30 minutes. Serves 4 to 6.

Spanish Rice

1½ cups long grain rice
½ cup olive oil, butter, or margarine
1 ½ cups tomato juice
1 ½ cups water
1 onion, chopped

1 green pepper, chopped
1½ teaspoons salt
1 pound hamburger or sausage, fried and drained (optional)

Saute raw rice in oil until golden brown. Place in pot with all remaining ingredients. Stir well. Cover and cook on LOW for 4 to 6 hours. (HIGH: 2 to 3 hours.) Serves 4 to 6.

Spanish Paella

1 3-pound chicken, cut up
2 cups water
1 cup long grain rice
2 cloves garlic, crushed
¼ cup olive oil or butter

¼ cup pimento, cut in strips
½ teaspoon oregano
½ teaspoon Spanish saffron
¾ pound raw shrimp
8- to 10-ounces clams or tuna

Cook chicken according to "Chicken In A Pot" recipe in Chapter 13, using 2 cups water and thinly sliced vegetables. Now, remove cooked chicken from broth, leaving broth and vegetables in pot. Bone chicken and cut meat into pieces. Return to pot. Next, in small skillet over medium heat, fry rice and garlic in olive oil or butter until rice is browned. Add to pot, along with all remaining ingredients. Stir together thoroughly. Cover and cook on LOW for 6 to 8 hours. (HIGH: 2 to 3 hours.) Serves 4 to 6.

Chapter Fourteen
Seafood

FROM THE briny deep, seafood is a joy to eat. You want to enjoy fish in many forms: in a stew, a chowder, as a main dish or a casserole. You want a minimum of preparation time, but you want it to taste as if hours and hours of work had gone into it.

All this is possible with your slow cooker. You can prepare almost any fish for any type of dish with the use of this crockery pot. Taste the rich goodness of fish from the seven seas with your slow cooker.

Curried Shrimp

1 small onion, finely chopped	1 to 2 teaspoons curry powder
2 cups cooked shrimp	1 can shrimp soup

1 cup dairy sour cream

Put all ingredients except sour cream in pot. Cover and cook on LOW 5 to 6 hours. Stir in sour cream. Heat and serve over rice. Serves 4 to 6.
SUGGESTION: Serve with curry condiments: chopped almonds, bacon crisps, boiled eggs.

Spiced Shrimp

1½ to 2 pounds fresh shrimp in shells
3 cups water or beer
1 tablespoon salt
1 packet shrimp spices or 1½ tablespoons mixed pickling spices

Put all ingredients in pot. Cover and cook on LOW 3 to 5 hours.
NOTE: If desired, fill pot with water or beer, salt, and spices; cook all day on LOW. Then turn to HIGH, add shrimp, and cook on HIGH 30 to 45 minutes or until shrimp turn pink. Serves 4 to 6.

Jiffy Lobster Newburg

1 cup shrimp soup
¾ cup evaporated milk (or cream)
2 egg yolks, beaten
5 ounces lobster, flaked
½ cup sliced mushrooms
2 tablespoons sherry

Place all ingredients in pot. Cook on HIGH and stir occasionally until soup is melted. Cover and cook on LOW 4 to 6 hours. Serve over hot rice, chow mein noodles or in puff pastry shells. Serves 4 to 6.
VARIATION FOR SHRIMP NEWBURG: For 1½ cups cooked and drained shrimp may be substituted for lobster.

Oyster Stew

1 quart milk
¼ cup margarine or butter
2 teaspoons salt
½ to 1 teaspoon Worcestershire sauce
2 tablespoons flour mixed with

2 tablespoons water (op-   1 pint oysters with liquid
tional)   Cayenne pepper

Put all ingredients except oysters in pot. (Use optional flour water paste for thicker soup.) Cover and cook on HIGH 1½ hours. Stir well. Add oysters and cook on LOW for 2 to 4 hours. Sprinkle with cayenne and serve hot. Serves 4 to 6.

Seafood Chowder

2 pounds fresh fish fillets (had-   2 cups water
dock, cod, etc.)   1½ teaspoons salt
¼ pound salt pork or bacon,   ¼ teaspoon pepper
diced   14 ounces evaporated milk
4 medium potatoes, pared and   1 medium onion, chopped
cubed

Thaw frozen fillets and cut into bite-size pieces. In small skillet, saute salt pork and onion until golden; drain and put into pot with fish. Add all remaining ingredients. Cover and cook on HIGH for 2 hours, then turn to LOW for 4 to 6 hours or until potatoes are tender. Serve in large bowls with crusty French bread. Serves 4 to 6.

Sherried Crab Meat

1½ cups crab meat   2 green onions with tops, finely
3 tablespoons butter   chopped
¼ cup dry sherry   Salt and pepper
¼ cup light cream
1 egg, beaten
10-ounces golden
mushroom or cream of
mushroom soup

Remove any cartilage or shell from crab meat; break into pieces and place in pot. Add all remaining ingredients. Stir gently. Cover and cook on HIGH for 1 hour, then on LOW for 4 to 6 hours. Serve over hot toast or in patty shells. Serves 4 to 6.

Rice 'N' Clams

¼ cup (½ stick) butter or margarine
1 small onion, finely chopped
1 stalk celery, finely chopped
1 cup long grain rice
2 cups chicken broth, or 2 cups water and 2 bouillon cubes

½ cup grated Parmesan cheese
⅔ cup ripe olives, chopped
1 cup shelled clams

Place all ingredients in pot. Stir well. Cover and cook on HIGH 1 hour, then on LOW 4 to 6 hours. Serves 4 to 6.

Salmon Cheese Casserole

1 pound salmon, with liquid
½ cup mushrooms
1½ cups bread crumbs

2 eggs, beaten
1 cup grated cheese
1 tablespoon lemon juice
1 tablespoon onion, minced

Flake fish in bowl, removing all bones. Add all remaining ingredients and mix thoroughly. Pour into lightly greased pot. Cover and cook on HIGH 1 hour, then turn to LOW for 3 to 4 hours. Serves 4 to 6.

Manhattan Clam Chowder

¼ pound salt pork or bacon, diced and fried
1 large onion, chopped
2 carrots, thinly sliced
3 stalks celery, sliced
1 tablespoon parsley flakes
1½ cup tomato wedges
1 ½ teaspoons salt

2 cups clams, shelled
2 whole peppercorns
1 bay leaf
1½ teaspoons dried thyme leaves, crushed
3 medium potatoes, pared and diced

Put all ingredients in pot. Cover and cook on HIGH 1 hour, then on LOW for 8 hours. Serves 4 to 6.

New England Clam Chowder: See recipe for Seafood Chowder in this chapter. Substitute 3 7-ounce cans of clams with their liquid for 2 pounds of fish.

Shrimp Creole

½ cup onions, chopped
½ cup celery, chopped
1 clove garlic, minced
3 tablespoons shortening
2 cups tomato wedges
1 cup tomato juice or sauce
1½ teaspoons salt
1 teaspoon sugar

½ tablespoon chili powder, or more to taste
1 tablespoon Worcestershire Sauce
Dash hot pepper sauce
2 tablespoons cornstarch
12-ounces shrimp
½ cup chopped green pepper

Cook onions, celery, and garlic in shortening in skillet until tender. Place in pot. Place tomatoes and sauce, spices, Worcestershire and hot pepper sauce in pot. Cover and cook on LOW for 4 to 6 hours. Add cornstarch to 1 tablespoon water and mix until smooth. Add to pot. Cook for 3 hours until thickened. Add shrimp and green pepper. Cook for one more hour. Serve with rice. Serves 4 to 6.

Chapter Fifteen
Soups and Sauces

THERE'S NOTHING like a good hearty soup. It may be a plain vegetable soup, or it may be more like a full meal in a bowl. You can enjoy many different soups with the use of your crockery pot. Let it do all the work for you. Then just enjoy the rewards of a good soup.

Sauces do much more than add flavor to foods. They bring out, they enhance, they amplify Nature's hidden tastes so that almost any food can become a gourmet treat if the sauce is right. And the best sauces require time and attention.

Now there's no need for you to labor for hours over a hot cookstove: just let your slow cooker prepare a savory sauce that will perfectly complement your foods.

Italian Meat Sauce

1 cup onion, chopped
1 to 1½ pounds ground chuck, extra lean
2 cloves garlic
2 pounds tomato wedges
1 cup tomato juice
6 ounces water (optional)
2 stalks celery with tops, chopped

2 teaspoons salt
3 teaspoons dried oregano, crushed
¼ teaspoon dried thyme, crushed
1 bay leaf

Put all ingredients in pot. Stir thoroughly. Cover and cook on LOW for 10 to 18 hours. (HIGH: 6 to 8 hours.) Serves 4 to 6.

Vegetable-Beef Soup

1 to 2 pounds beef shanks, ox-tails, short ribs, or veal bones
1 pound of tomatoes
2 carrots, sliced
3 stalks celery with tops, sliced
2 medium onions, diced
2 medium potatoes, diced

3 cups water
1 teaspoon salt
4 peppercorns
3 beef bouillon cubes
10 ounces of your favorite vegetables.

Put all ingredients in pot. Cover and cook on LOW for 12 to 24 hours. (HIGH: 7 to 10 hours.) Serves 4 to 6.
*May be added during last 2 hours of cooking.

French Onion Soup

1 quart beef bouillon or brown stock
3 cups yellow onions, thinly sliced
¼ cup butter
1½ teaspoons salt

¼ cup sugar (helps onions to brown)
2 tablespoons flour
¼ cup dry vermouth or cognac (optional)
1 cup grated Parmesan cheese

Pour bouillon or stock into pot; cover and set on HIGH. Cook onions slowly in large skillet in butter; cover and let cook for about 15 minutes. Uncover and add salt, sugar, and flour. Stir well. Add to stock in pot. Cover and cook on LOW 6 to 8 hours. (HIGH: 3 hours.) Serves 4 to 6.

Ham and Lima Beans

1 pound dry lima beans,
   soaked overnight in water
   to cover
1 large onion, chopped
1 large green pepper
1 teaspoon dry mustard

1 teaspoon salt
1 teaspoon pepper
¼ to ½ pound ham or bacon,
   cut in small pieces
1 cup water
1 cup tomato juice

Put all ingredients in pot. Stir together well. Cover and cook on LOW for 7 to 10 hours. (HIGH: 4 to 5 hours.) Serve with wedges of hot corn bread. Serves 4 to 6.

"Home Made" Potato Soup

6 potatoes, peeled and cut into
   bite-size pieces
2 leeks, washed and cut into
   bite-size pieces (optional)
2 onions, chopped
1 carrot, pared and sliced
4 chicken bouillon cubes
1 stalk celery, sliced

1 tablespoon parsley flakes
5 cups water
1 tablespoon salt
Pepper
⅓ cup butter
1 can evaporated milk
Chives, chopped

Put all ingredients except chives in pot. Cover and cook on LOW 10 to 12 hours. If desired, mash potatoes with masher before serving. Serve topped with chopped chives. Serves 4 to 6.

Cheese Soup

20-ounces cream soup (celery,
   mushroom or chicken)

1 cup milk
1 pound Cheddar cheese, cubed

¼ teaspoon paprika
Croutons

Put all ingredients except croutons in pot. Cover and cook on LOW for 4 to 6 hours. (HIGH: 2 hours, stirring occasionally.) Serve in warm bowls; top each serving with crisp croutons. Serves 4 to 6.

Garbure Basque (Ham and bean soup with vegetables)

1 pound dry Navy or pea
   beans, soaked overnight in
   water to cover
4 cups water
1 2-to 3-pound ham butt
1 onion, sliced
2 cloves garlic, chopped
1 green pepper, cut into strips

1 hot pepper (optional)
10 ounces limas
10 ounces peas
1 carrot, sliced
½ small head cabbage,
   shredded
Salt and pepper

Place all ingredients *except* vegetables and cabbage in pot. Cover and cook on LOW 12 to 18 hours. Turn to HIGH and remove ham. Add peas, limas, and cabbage. Cook for 1 to 2 hours on HIGH or until vegetables are tender. Serve large bowls of this thick soup with crusty French bread. Serves 4 to 6.

Dutch Pea Soup

1 pound pigs' feet (about 12)
¼ pound shin beef
¼ pound fresh "fat back"
   bacon
½ pound split peas
1 small bunch celery with root,
   chopped

2 leeks, white part only,
   cleaned and cut up
3 cups water
Salt and pepper to taste

Place all ingredients except seasoning in pot. Cover and cook on

HIGH for one hour. Reduce heat to LOWand cook for 10 to 12 hours. Remove pigs' feet, bacon, and beef. Whirl the remainder of the soup in blender, holding top firmly in place, or press mixture through sieve or food mill. Add pigs' feet, bacon, and beef. Place back in pot for one hour to reheat. Serves 4 to 6.

Chicken With Rice Soup

1½ pounds chicken necks
3 carrots, sliced
2 stalks celery with ends, sliced
2 onions, diced
1 bay leaf
2 teaspoons salt

1 teaspoon pepper
1 teaspoon oregano
2 teaspoons parsley
4 cups water
1 cup cooked rice

Add all ingredients, except rice, to pot. Cover and set on LOW. Cook for 8 to 12 hours. Add cooked rice during last ½ hour of cooking, and serve. Serves 4 to 6.

Lentil-Vegetable Soup

2 cups lentils, soaked overnight, drained, and sorted
5 cups water
2 slices bacon, diced
1 medium onion, chopped
1 carrot, thinly sliced
2 stalks celery with tops, sliced

1 garlic clove, minced
2½ teaspoons salt
¼ teaspoon pepper
½ teaspoon dried oregano,
crushed
1 pound tomatoes
2 tablespoons wine vinegar

Put all ingredients in pot. Mix together well. Cover and cook on LOW 8 to 10 hours. Before serving, season to taste. Serves 4 to 6.

Split Pea Soup

Follow recipe for Old-Fashioned Bean Soup, in Chapter 4, substituting 1 pound dry green split peas for dry Navy beans. Soak split peas in water before cooking. Serves 4 to 6.

Minestrone

1 quart (4 cups) water
2 to 3 pounds beef shank
1 to 2 pounds marrow beef bones (2 or 3 bones — optional)
1 medium onion, diced
2 carrots, diced
2 stalks celery with tops, sliced
1 cup diced leeks (optional)
1 pound tomato wedges
10 ounces of your favorite vegetables
2 teaspoons salt
1 zucchini, sliced
1 cup shredded cabbage
1 tablespoon dried basil
1 clove garlic, minced
½ cup vermicelli or a 1 pound can garbanzo beans
1 teaspoon oregano

One day in advance, prepare the stock: place water, beef shank, and marrow bones in pot. Cover and cook overnight (8 to 12 hours) on LOW. Remove meat and bones from liquid. Cool. Scoop marrow from bones and return lean meat to stock. (Can be done in advance and refrigerated.) Add all remaining ingredients to 2 cups stock in pot. Cover and cook on HIGH 1 hour, then on LOW 6 to 8 hours. (HIGH: 4 hours.) Ladle into bowls and sprinkle with Parmesan cheese. Serve with crusty French bread. Serves 4 to 6.

All-Meat Chili Spread

4 pounds ground chuck
3 cups water
3 cloves garlic, minced
1 tablespoon salt
2 to 3 tablespoons cumin
4 to 6 tablespoons chili powder

Brown chuck to remove excess fat (or skim fat off top before serving). Put all ingredients in pot; stir thoroughly to mix spices. Cover and cook on HIGH for 2 hours, stir well and turn to LOW for 6 to 10 hours. Serve topped with fresh chopped onions. Serves 4 to 6.

Meat Sauce For Pasta

½ pound mushrooms, sliced
1 clove garlic, crushed
2 medium onions, chopped
1½ pounds chopped chuck
1 pound tomato puree
2½ tablespoons tomato paste, or more if thicker sauce is desired

½ cup dry red wine
1 teaspoon salt
½ teaspoon pepper
1½ tablespoons oregano
1 bay leaf
Pinch of basil
½ teaspoon sugar

Saute mushrooms in butter. Saute onions and garlic in some oil in frypan until lightly browned. Add meat, stirring until crumbly, and it loses its pink color. Place mushrooms, meat, and all other ingredients in pot. Cover and cook on LOW for 6 to 10 hours. Serve over spaghetti or noodles with grated cheese, or use as a sauce for Italian casseroles.

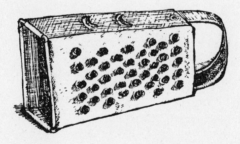

Chapter Sixteen
Vegetables

PEOPLE WON'T turn up their noses at vegetables when they discover the true, delicate flavor of vegetables from the slow cooker. How can this be possible? Your slow cooker "knows" how to steam with a minimum of liquid so that vegetables taste as good as Nature wanted them to be.

When vegetables are cooked by your crockery pot, they can become winning favorites on your family's dinner table. You'll love them, too!

Hearty Vegetable Stew

2 medium onions, diced 3 carrots, sliced
1 clove garlic, crushed 1 cup tomato puree
2 cups cabbage, finely grated 1 beef or chicken stock cube

3 tablespoons oil
1 bay leaf
1 tablespoon oregano
1 quart water

Salt and pepper to taste
2 cups medium egg noodles
1 pound chicken necks, or 3
soup bones (optional)

Saute onions and garlic in oil in skillet. Add all ingredients to pot, except noodles. Cover and cook on LOW for 12 to 18 hours. Cook noodles according to package directions and add to pot during last half-hour of cooking. Serves 6 to 8.

Candied Carrots

6 to 8 carrots, pared and cut in
1-inch pieces
½ teaspoon salt
1½ tablespoons cornstarch, dissolved in 2 tablespoons water

2 tablespoons brown sugar, or
to taste
1½ tablespoons butter or
margarine

Place carrots and 1 cup water in pot. Cook on HIGH for 6 to 8 hours, until carrots are tender. Add butter to carrot water and melt. Add remaining ingredients and cook for 1 to 1½ hours, stirring occasionally, until gravy thickens. Serves 4 to 6.

Broccoli with Lemon/Garlic Sauce

1 head broccoli, broken into
flowerets
1 teaspoon salt

Water to cover broccoli
Lemon/Garlic Sauce*

Place all ingredients in pot. Cover and cook on HIGH for 2 to 3 hours until tender. Serve with Lemon   Garlic Sauce. Serves 4.

*Lemon/Garlic Sauce:
5 tablespoons butter or
margarine
2 small cloves garlic, pressed

1 teaspoon lemon juice
Dash salt

Melt butter in small saucepan—do not burn. Add all ingredients and keep warm over very low flame on stove. Serve over broccoli.

Cauliflower with Cheese Sauce

1 cauliflower, broken into
   flowerets
1 teaspoon salt

Water to cover cauliflower
Cheese Sauce*

Place all ingredients in pot. Cover and set on HIGH. Cook for 2 to 4 hours, until tender. Serve with Cheese Sauce. Serves 4.

*Cheese Sauce:
1½ cups milk
2 tablespoons cornstarch mixed
   with 2 tablespoons water

⅓ cup grated Parmesan cheese
Salt and pepper

Combine milk and cornstarch mixture in a saucepan, and heat on stove until thickened. Add cheese. Season with salt and pepper. Serve over hot vegetables.

Fresh or Frozen Vegetables

Use two 10-ounce packages of frozen vegetables, or cleaned ready-to-cook fresh vegetables. Cover and cook on HIGH for 45 minutes, then on LOW 2 to 4 hours. Stir occasionally. (Vegetables may be wrapped in foil to eliminate stirring.) Serves 3 to 5.
Suggested Vegetables: Potatoes, broccoli spears, asparagus, cauliflower, artichokes.
NOTE: Add ½ cup water, except for artichokes which should have 2 cups of water.

Baked Potatoes

Fill pot with scrubbed and well-greased potatoes. Cover and cook on LOW 8 to 10 hours. Do not add water.

Baked Sweet Potatoes

Place washed, unpeeled sweet potatoes in pot. Add about ¼ cup water. Cover and cook on HIGH 1 hour, then turn to LOW for 6 to 8 hours or until potatoes are tender.

Fresh Green Beans

2 pounds fresh green beans, washed and cut up
3 to 4 cups water

1 teaspoon salt
¼ pound ham or bacon pieces

Put all ingredients in pot. Cover and cook on LOW for 10 to 24 hours. (HIGH: 6 to 10 hours.) Stir occasionally.

Acorn Squash

Place whole rinsed squash in pot. Cook as for Sweet Potatoes in this chapter. Split and remove seeds when cooked; sprinkle with salt and cinnamon, and dot with butter. (May be split and wrapped with foil before baking.)

Fresh Corn On The Cob

Remove silks but leave green outer husks on the ears and cut off ends so corn will fit in pot in standing position. Wash thoroughly. Put six to eight ears in pot. Cover and cook on HIGH 45 minutes, then turn to LOW for 1½ to 2 hours. Remove husks and serve.

Bavarian Red Cabbage

1 small head red cabbage, washed and coarsely sliced
1 medium onion, chopped
3 tart apples, cored and quartered

2 teaspoons salt
1 cup hot water
1½ tablespoons sugar
½ cup vinegar
3 tablespoons bacon grease or butter

Put all ingredients in pot in order listed. Cover and cook on LOW for 8 to 10 hours. (HIGH: 3 hours.) Stir well before serving. Excellent served with a rich meat. Serves 4 to 6.

Artichokes

4 to 6 artichokes
Salt

Melted butter and lemon juice
or Sauterne Sauce*

Wash and trim artichokes. Cut off about 1 inch from top and, if desired, trim tips of leaves. Stand upright in pot. Add ¼ teaspoon salt for each artichoke and 2 tablespoons lemon juice. Pour in 2 cups hot water. Cover and cook on LOW 6 to 8 hours. Serve with melted butter and lemon, or with Sauterne Sauce. Serves 4 to 6.

*Sauterne Sauce:

1 cup sauterne
3 tablespoons minced onion
2 cups mayonnaise (1 pint)

3 tablespoons parsley ffft, beaten

Mix well and heat slowly. Dip artichoke leaves and hearts into sauce.

Chapter Seventeen
Wild Game

YOUR CROCKERY pot is superior to most other types of appliances for cooking wild game. This is because of its thorough, very slow cooking that permits no evaporation.

Game that is properly prepared, stored, and soaked in a marinade prior to cooking will defy detection as "wild." Marinade imparts good flavor to game without adding any distinctive taste of its own. Yes, your crockery pot is a "natural" for large or small game and upland birds. To match the flavor of beef and domestic fowl, game *must* be cooked slowly...and this is your pot's unique specialty!

Game aficionados have expressed high praise for meats and birds cooked in the crockery pot. You will, too. Just remember—*game must be thoroughly cooked.* Better to allow more time than necessary; never allow less time than is called for in these recipes.

Marinade No. 1
(A popular standby for all game foods)

½ cup vinegar

2 cloves garlic, minced

2 tablespoons salt

Cold water to cover game

Mix ingredients together in bowl just large enough to cover game with water. Soak frozen or fresh game overnight. No need to stir this marinade. Use for red meat or game birds.

Marinade No. 2

1 cup dry vermouth

½ cup brandy

½ cup peanut oil

3 tablespoons fresh lemon juice

1 bay leaf, crumbled

Water

Mix ingredients thoroughly. Soak small pieces of meat or thin slices at least 2 hours, stirring marinade frequently. Marinate large cuts or whole birds overnight (stir often, or marinade will separate). Be sure game is covered completely with marinade—use at least two cups water with preceding recipe, more if needed.

Venison Stew

2 pounds venison stew meat, cut in 1-inch cubes

Salt and pepper

2 tablespoons butter or oil

3 stalks celery, cut diagonally in 1-inch pieces

½ cup chopped onion

2 cloves garlic, minced

1 tablespoon chopped parsley

⅓ cup water

⅓ cup dry red wine

1 8-ounce cup tomato sauce

1 9-ounce package frozen artichoke hearts (optional)

Salt and pepper venison cubes. Brown lightly in 2 tablespoons butter.

or oil. Put celery and onion in pot. Add browned meat cubes and remaining ingredients. Cover and cook on LOW for 7 to 12 hours. (HIGH: 4 to 6 hours, stirring occasionally.) Serve over rice or buttered noodles. Serves 4 to 6.

Pheasant With Wild Rice Stuffing

2 stalks celery, cut in 2-inch pieces
1 3-pound, ready-to-cook pheasant
2 tablespoons butter or margarine
¾ cup celery, diced
½ cup onion, chopped
2 tablespoons parsley, chopped
1 teaspoon salt
¼ teaspoon pepper
¾ teaspoon rosemary (optional)
½ cup sliced mushrooms
1½ cups wild rice, cooked
10 ounces cream of mushroom or cream of chicken soup, undiluted
2 cup sauterne or milk

Place celery pieces in bottom of pot as "flavor rack" for pheasant. Rinse pheasant and pat dry with paper towel. Now prepare stuffing. In medium skillet, melt butter and saute diced celery, onion and parsley until lightly browned, about 10 minutes. Add remaining ingredients except soup and sauterne or milk. Mix together thoroughly.

Spoon stuffing lightly into neck and cavity of pheasant. Truss pheasant with skewers. Place bird with breast down on celery pieces in pot. Pour in soup which has been mixed with sauterne or milk. Cover and cook on LOW for 6 to 8 hours. (HIGH: 2½ to 3½ hours.) Remove pheasant carefully with metal spatula to serving platter. Serve with the sauce poured over roast pheasant and rice stuffing. Serves 4 to 6.

Venison—Rabbit—Squirrel—Duck

3 to 4 pounds game meat (Very fresh or frozen)
Marinade (See listings in this chapter)
1 large onion, cut up
½ large green pepper, cut up
1 to 2 stalks celery, sliced
2 cloves garlic, chopped
Salt and pepper to taste
½ teaspoon oregano

1 tablespoon dry parsley, or
several fresh sprigs
3 tablespoons of
tomato sauce

Cayenne pepper to taste
1 cup liquid (sauterne, cider,
tomato sauce, or water)

Soak fresh or frozen meat overnight in marinade. Cut meat into serving-size pieces and brown with vegetables in hot skillet 5 to 10 minutes. Place all meat and other ingredients in pot. Cover and cook on LOW 8 to 10 hours. Serves 4 to 6.

Roast Wild Duck

Soak one large duck or 2 mallards in marinade overnight (See listing in this chapter for marinades). Season inside and out with salt and pepper. Brown well in lightly oiled skillet to remove excess fat. Stuff each cavity with 2 chopped potatoes, 2 chopped carrots and 2 chopped apples (this stuffing, *discarded after cooking*, absorbs unwanted fat and wild flavor). Place 2 sliced carrots in bottom of pot to act as rack for bird(s). Put stuffed duck(s) in pot. Add ½ cup sauterne, dry vermouth, or water. Cover and cook on HIGH 2 hours, then turn to LOW for 8 hours. Before serving, remove chopped vegetables from each cavity. Serve with rice, baked sweet potatoes, or potatoes. Serves 4 to 6.
NOTE: If ducks have been skinned, pin 2 bacon strips across each breast and place under broiler for 10 to 15 minutes before serving.

Roast Venison

1 4-pound venison roast
2 tablespoons flour
2 cloves garlic, minced
1 large onion, sliced

2 tablespoons brown sugar
¼ cup vinegar or lemon juice
1 pound tomato wedges

Allow fresh or frozen venison to stand overnight in a marinade (See listing in this chapter). Season with salt, roll in flour, and brown in hot skillet. Place in pot. Add remaining ingredients. Cover and cook on HIGH for 2 hours, then turn to LOW for 8 to 10 hours. Serves 4 to 6.

Chapter Eighteen
What's For Dessert?"

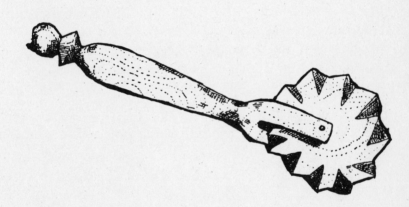

IN DAYS gone by, desserts were treats at the end of a luscious homemade meal. Many a cook worked for hours over a hot stove to prepare a simple dessert that would delight all those who enjoyed its good taste. Today, thanks to the crockery pot slow cooker, there is no need to labor for hours to enjoy a homemade dessert. Let the crockery pot do most of the work while you and your family do most of the enjoying of the desserts.

Honeyed Rhubarb

4 cups rhubarb in ½ inch pieces	1 cup sugar, or to taste ¼ teaspoon salt

3 tablespoons flour

2 tablespoons grated lemon rind

⅓ cup strained honey

2 tablespoons butter or margarine

1 cup water

Add all ingredients to pot. Cover and cook on LOW 10 to 12 hours, until rhubarb is tender. Add more sugar to taste. Serve warm with cream (or use as pie filling). Serves 4 to 6.

Rice Pudding

2½ cups cooked rice

1½ cups scalded milk

⅔ cup brown or white sugar

3 tablespoons soft butter or margarine

2 teaspoons vanilla

½ to 1 teaspoon nutmeg or cinnamon

3 eggs, beaten

¾ cup raisins (optional)

Combine all ingredients in lightly greased pot; cover. Cook on HIGH for 1 to 2 hours, stirring occasionally during first ½ hour of cooking. Serves 6.

Applesauce

5 pounds cooking apples

1 cup water

2 cinnamon sticks

2 cups sugar

Peel and quarter apples. Place in pot with water and sugar. Cover and cook on LOW for 4 to 6 hours until tender. Stir occasionally. Puree apples through food mill or sieve. Place puree and cinnamon sticks back in cooker. Cook on LOW for 2 more hours, stirring occasionally for best flavor. Makes 8 cups.

Steamed Fig Pudding

¼ cup butter

1 cup molasses

½ cup milk
2 cups figs, chopped
4 eggs, separated
2 cups flour

½ teaspoon salt
1 teaspoon baking powder
½ teaspoon soda

Melt butter. Add molasses, milk and figs. Beat egg yolks well and add. Stir in unsifted dry ingredients. Beat egg whites until stiff and cut into the original mixture. Place in a 2-quart buttered pudding mold and cover with aluminum foil. Add 3 cups of water to pot and place mold in it, being certain that the water will not leak into mold during cooking. Cover and cook on LOW for 9 to 10 hours. Serve with hard sauce or vanilla ice cream. Serves 4.

Spiced Prunes

1 pound prunes (about 42)
4 cups water
⅓ cup vinegar
⅓ cup dark brown sugar

3 sticks cinnamon
1 tablespoon whole cloves, in cheesecloth bag

Combine all ingredients in pot. Cook on LOW for 2 to 3 hours. Remove cloves. Prunes will keep in refrigerator for several weeks. Serve as relish or garnish for meat or poultry.

Steamed Chocolate Pudding

1½ teaspoons butter
⅓ cup sugar
1 egg
½ cup milk
2 cups and 2 teaspoons flour, sifted

2 teaspoons baking powder
Dash salt
1¼ ounces (1¼ squares) cooking chocolate

Cream butter and sugar and add egg. Mix well. Sift dry ingredients and add alternately with milk. Melt chocolate and stir in. Grease a mold or

1-pound coffee can, pour in dough and cover with foil. Pour 2½ cups water into pot. Place mold in. Cover. Cook on HIGH for 2 to 3 hours. Serve warm with cream or hard sauce. Serves 6.

Hard Sauce

⅓ cup butter or margarine

1 cup confectioners' sugar

½ teaspoon orange extract

1 teaspoon vanilla extract

Cream butter or margarine while gradually adding confectioners' sugar, beating continually. Add extracts and serve over dessert. Makes ⅔cup.

Buttery Cinnamon Baked Apples

7 to 8 medium cooking apples

2 tablespoons raisins or currants

¼ cup brown sugar

1 tablespoon cinnamon

½ teaspoon butter per apple

Wash and core apples. Mix raisins with sugar and pack mixture into apple centers. Sprinkle with cinnamon. Add ½ teaspoon butter to each apple. Place apples in pot with ½ cup water. Cover. Cook on LOW for 7 to 9 hours. Serve warm with cream. Serves 6 to 8.

Indian Pudding

⅓ cup stone-ground yellow cornmeal

3 tablespoons skim milk powder

4 cups boiling milk

1 cup dark molasses

2 tablespoons safflower oil

½ teaspoon cinnamon

½ teaspoon ginger

½ cup raisins

2 eggs, well beaten

1 cup cold milk

Cook cornmeal with skim milk powder in boiling milk in double boiler. Stir constantly, cooking 15 to 20 minutes. Stir in dark molasses, safflower oil, cinnamon, ginger, and raisins. Add the well-beaten eggs and pour mixture into well-greased pot. Pour cold milk over mixture but do not stir. Cook on LOW for 4 to 6 hours. Serve with ice cream or heavy cream. Serves 4.

Spicy Pumpkin Pie Filling

How To Cook Raw Pumpkin: Cut 3 pound raw pumpkin in half. Remove seeds and stringy portion. Cut in small pieces and peel. Place in cooker in 3 inches of water. Cover and cook on HIGH for 8 to 9 hours until pumpkin is tender. Drain and run through food mill or sieve. Makes 3 cups.

Tawny Pie Filling:

2 eggs, lightly beaten
2 cups pumpkin
¾ cup sugar
½ teaspoon salt
1 teaspoon ground cinnamon

½ teaspoon ground ginger
¼ teaspoon ground cloves
1⅔ cups light cream or
    evaporated milk

Blend eggs and pumpkin. Blend in remaining ingredients and fill pie shell. Makes 1 large pumpkin pie.

Baked Apple Tapioca

5 cups cooking apples, peeled
    and sliced
2½ cups water
¼ teaspoon ground cloves
½ cup quick-cooking tapioca
½ cup red cinnamon candies
    ("red-hots")

½ cup sugar
½ teaspoon salt
¼ cup butter
¼ cup lemon juice

Arrange apples in well-greased pot. Combine water, cloves, tapioca, candies, sugar and salt and bring to boil over medium heat in saucepan, stirring constantly. Continue cooking at rapid boil for 1 minute. Remove from heat, add butter and lemon juice, and stir until butter melts. Pour mixture over apples in pot. Cover and cook on LOW for 6 to 8 hours, or until apples are tender. Serve warm with whipped cream or vanilla ice cream, with or without a sprinkling of cinnamon. Serves 4 to 6.

Butterscotch Bread Pudding

3 cups milk, scalded
1½ cups bread, cubed
¾ cup brown sugar
3 tablespoons melted butter

2 eggs, slightly beaten
¼ teaspoon salt
1 teaspoon vanilla
½ teaspoon almond extract

Generously grease pot. Pour scalded milk into bowl with bread. Allow to cool. Cook brown sugar with butter in pan, stirring until melted; add to milk and bread. Add remaining ingredients. Blend and turn into greased pot. Cover and cook on LOW for 3 to 4 hours. Serves 4.

Illustrations by Tom Keynton